THE MASK OF RELIGION

When Peter Fleck left the Plainfield, N.J., area in 1974 he had been an active member of the First Unitarian Society of Plainfield for nearly thirty years. He has been our lay preacher, mentor to ever-changing boards of trustees, officiator at weddings and memorial services, and oftentimes "minister without frock" to some of our troubled members. With his wife, Ruth, at his side he has always been available to us in time of need.

Many of us who have been influenced by his preaching feel that his religious insights and perspectives should reach a wider congregation. We hope this book will serve that purpose.

BOARD OF TRUSTEES,
First Unitarian Society of Plainfield, New Jersey

THE MASK

OF

RELIGION

※

G. PETER FLECK

PROMETHEUS BOOKS
BUFFALO, NEW YORK

Excerpts on pages 4 to 5 from J.B., A PLAY IN VERSE, by Archibald MacLeish (Copyright © 1956, 1957, 1958 by Archibald MacLeish). Reprinted by permission of the publisher, Houghton Mifflin.

Lines on page 65 from *Collected Poems, 1909–1962* by T. S. Eliot (Copyright © 1963 by Thomas Stearns Eliot). Reprinted by permission of Harcourt Brace Jovanivich.

Lines on page 107 from THE POETRY OF ROBERT FROST edited by Edward Connery Lathem. Copyright © 1962 by Robert Frost. Copyright © 1969 by Holt, Rinehart and Winston. Reprinted by permission of Holt, Rinehart and Winston, Publishers.

Excerpts, on pages 120 to 121, abridged from pp. 98–100 in OUR TOWN: A PLAY IN THREE ACTS by Thornton Wilder. Copyright © 1938, 1957 by Thornton Wilder. By permission of Harper & Row, Publishers, Inc. and Isabel Wilder.

The author has assigned the proceeds from this book to the First Unitarian Society of Plainfield, New Jersey.

Published 1980 by Prometheus Books
1203 Kensington Avenue
Buffalo, New York 14215

Library of Congress Catalogue Number: 79-9644
ISBN 0-87975-125-8
Printed in the United States of America
Second printing

To Mort, without whom there would
have been no sermons

To Jeannette, without whom there would
have been no book

To Ruth, who, as usual, made it all
possible

Acknowledgments

I am grateful to Vincent R. Stafford of the First Unitarian Society of Plainfield, N.J., who took the initiative of suggesting this book; to Agnes Hannay for her encouragement, and to Dorothy Howell-Thomas, Robert Kruseman, Dr. Max Kohnstamm, and Stanley Goldman for making valuable suggestions.

I would also like to thank the Reverend Neil W. Gerdes, Librarian of the Meadville/Lombard Theological School, Chicago, who was helpful in providing bibliographic information; Roberta Leighton, who copy edited this book; Dennis O'Donnell, who assisted in verifying citations; Sidney Feinberg, who designed the book; Janet Halverson, who designed the jacket; and Margaret Gilmore for her competence in typing the manuscript.

Above all, I want to thank the members of the First Unitarian Society of Plainfield, N.J. for their friendship.

Contents

IV. TRANSFORMING

When the great Rabbi Israel Baal Shem-Tov saw misfortune threatening the Jews it was his custom to go into a certain part of the forest to meditate. There he would light a fire, say a special prayer, and the miracle would be accomplished and the misfortune averted.

Later, when his disciple, the celebrated Magid of Mezritch, had occasion, for the same reason, to intercede with heaven, he would go to the same place in the forest and say: "Master of the Universe, listen! I do not know how to light the fire, but I am still able to say the prayer," and again the miracle would be accomplished.

Still later, Rabbi Moshe-Leib of Sasov, in order to save his people once more, would go into the forest and say: "I do not know how to light the fire, I do not know the prayer, but I know the place and this must be sufficient." It was sufficient and the miracle was accomplished.

Then it fell to Rabbi Israel of Rizhyn to overcome misfortune. Sitting in his armchair, his head in his hands, he spoke to God: "I am unable to light the fire and I do not know the prayer; I cannot even find the place in the forest. All I can do is to tell the story, and this must be sufficient." And it was sufficient.[1]

ELIE WIESEL, *The Gates of the Forest*

[1] Notes are on pages 187–197.

I

KNOWING

1

%%%

The Mask of Religion

Again there was a day when the sons of God came to present themselves before the Lord, and Satan came also among them. . . .

And the Lord said unto Satan, Whence comest thou? And Satan answered the Lord, and said, From going to and fro in the earth, and from walking up and down in it.

And the Lord said unto Satan, Hast thou considered my servant Job, that there is none like him in the earth, a perfect and an upright man, one that feareth God, and escheweth evil? and still he holdeth fast his integrity, although thou movedst me against him, to destroy him without cause.

JOB 2:1–3

The drive of our conscious life . . . is such that it makes belief in God plausible. Indeed, in many ways it leads us to act *as if* there were a God.

MICHAEL NOVAK, *A Time to Build*[1]

In his play *J.B.,* Archibald MacLeish presents a modern version of the Job story. In its modernness he reveals its timelessness. He presents it as a play within a play.

Two down-and-out, elderly actors, revealingly named Mr. Zuss and Nickles, who make a living as circus vendors, the one by selling balloons, the other by selling popcorn, stumble after hours onto a deserted stage in an empty circus tent. Apparently the Job story has been performed before they entered; the props, including masks for the actors impersonating God and Satan, are still lying around. After some hesita-

[3]

tion the two men begin to act out the play before an imaginary audience.

They take their places back to back.
[Mr. Zuss:]   Masks!
They raise their masks to their faces.
                     Lights!
The bulbs go out. Darkness. Silence. In the silence:

A Distant Voice:	*Whence comest thou?*
Mr. Zuss:	That's my line.
Nickles:	I didn't speak it.
Mr. Zuss:	You did. Stop your mischief, won't you?
Nickles:	Stop your own! . . . .
Mr. Zuss:	Lights, I said!

The spotlight throws the enormous shadows on the canvas sky.

Godmask:	*Whence comest thou?*
Satanmask:	*From going to and fro in the earth . . .*
	And from walking up and down in it. . . .[2]

And then the play within the play begins, the story of J.B., the modern Job. When J.B. has lost everything and still blesses the name of the Lord, the play within the play is interrupted. Mr. Zuss and Nickles discuss the dramatic events they have witnessed. They wonder how it all will end.

Mr. Zuss: Well,
         We still have time to see.
Nickles: Put on your
         Mask! You'll see!

The light has faded but the faces of the actors are still visible.

Mr. Zuss: *(raising his mask)*   Put on your own!

Nickles leans over to find it, searching the floor of the platform with his hands. A long silence. From the silence at length:

The Distant Voice:	*Hast thou considered my servant Job*
	That there is none like him on the earth,
	A perfect and an upright man, one
	That feareth God and escheweth evil?
Nickles:	Wait a minute! I can't find . . .
The Distant Voice:	*(louder)*
	And still he holdeth fast his integrity . . .
Nickles:	Wait a minute, can't you? What the . . .
The Distant Voice:	*(almost a whisper)*
	Although thou movedst me against him
	To destroy him . . .

Nickles rises, his mask in his two hands. He wheels on Mr. Zuss only to see that Mr. Zuss also has his mask in his hands and stands staring up into the canvas sky.

(The Distant Voice is barely audible.)

without cause . . .

Silence. The two old actors stand side by side, holding their masks, their heads moving slowly together as they search the dark.

Nickles: Who said that?

Silence.

Mr. Zuss:	They want us to go on.
Nickles:	Why don't you?
Mr. Zuss:	He was asking *you*.
Nickles:	Who was?
Mr. Zuss:	He was.
Nickles:	Prompter probably. Prompter somewhere.[3]

Is there a Prompter somewhere?

Mircea Eliade tells us about a ritual observed by the Mord-

[5]

vin, a primitive Eastern European tribe. "It was . . . customary," he writes, "for an old man to symbolize the god Nishkipaz. He would climb onto the roof of a hut or into a tree, and when the people called upon him: Nishkipaz, give us grain! the old man would shout from above: 'I will.' "[4]

For me this story has a strange fascination. I have been wondering about the feelings of that old man, sitting on the roof of that hut or in that tree impersonating the god Nishkipaz, and about the feelings of the people gathered around that hut or that tree, looking up to him and praying for the blessing of a good harvest. Did they believe that the old man had somehow become God? I don't think so. They knew perfectly well that the guy up there was old Joe. And what about the old man? Did he believe that he was God? I don't think so. Still, I surmise that he would proclaim the words "I will" with great solemnity, that he would make his promise of a good harvest with the conviction that in making it he was somehow bringing about its fulfillment by the powers of the God he was impersonating.

Impersonating: the word is derived from the latin *persona,* and *persona* means mask, the mask worn on the stage by the actors of antiquity. Literally it means, therefore, that the old man put on the mask of God, that he was acting out God's role, that he was playing God.

There is a stunning analogy between this Stone Age ritual of the old man sitting on the roof top and that twentieth-century rendering of the Job story in which it is not clear whether the players play their parts upon the urging of the Distant Voice or whether in playing their parts the players evoke the Distant Voice. In both cases an ordinary human being placed in an elevated position—Mr. Zuss, in *J.B.,* according to the stage directions, stands on a wooden platform

of six or seven feet—impersonates God, puts on the *persona,*
the mask, of God, in the Stone Age case figuratively speaking,
in the twentieth-century case literally speaking.

The difference is important; it spells the end of the analogy.
In the earlier case man could play his God role openly, face
to face. Modern man can speak God language only from
behind a mask, a mask that protects him from the embarrassment of a face-to-face exposure, a mask that masks his self-
consciousness, his basic doubt, his lack of faith.

But it goes deeper than that. In the last of six talks Leonard
Bernstein gave at Harvard in 1973, he said:

We tend to view our century as so advanced, so prosperous and
swift in its developments, that we lose sight of its deeper, truer
self-image, the image of a shy, frightened child adrift in a shaky
universe, living under the constant threat of Mummy and Daddy
about to divorce or die. And so we must cover up, we must hide
our profound embarrassment at direct emotional expression; we
can no longer say, like Schubert: Du bist die Ruh [thou art still-
ness], just like that, or like Matthew Arnold: "Ah, love, let us
be true to one another!" We cannot afford that luxury; we're too
scared. . . . Between the nineteenth and twentieth centuries
"falls the shadow," as Eliot said. The new century must speak
through a mask. . . . It is the obliquity of expression that is now
semantically paramount; aesthetic perceptions are registered at a
remove; they are, so to speak, heard around a corner.[5]

What Leonard Bernstein says about aesthetic perceptions
applies with equal force to religious perceptions. Most of us
—at least most of us liberals—can no longer say: "I believe
in God"; we can no longer speak of "the good Father" who
"knows what you need." How can we in the age of Social
Security and pension funds quote with a straight face from
the Sermon on the Mount, "Take . . . no thought for the

morrow: for the morrow shall take thought for the things of itself," or square our acquisitive instincts with the admonition "lay not up for [yourselves] treasures upon earth"? How can we in the age of Auschwitz and Hiroshima rely on the assurance that "the very hairs of [your] head are all numbered" and give credence to the words of the psalmist, "Yea, though I walk through the valley of the shadow of death, I will fear no evil"? The answer is that we cannot. Or at least not with integrity. We liberals can speak of these things only —again in the words of Bernstein—"hiding behind the mask of once directly expressed emotion."[6]

But, you may ask, as I have, why then speak of these things at all? Why not forget about the whole religious business?

There is a very simple answer to this question: Let those who can forget, forget. Many of us cannot forget these things, for they represent the myth into which we were born, the myth of which we are a part. Yes, they make up that myth— and I use the word "myth" here as the emotional, religious, philosophical, ethical system in which we are nourished and which alone encompasses the historical memory of the race. If we could forget, why would Stravinsky and so many other modern composers still compose masses; why would Rouault and so many other modern painters still paint Christ; why would Anne Sexton and so many other modern poets still write poems celebrating him?

We cannot forget these things; we experience the need to speak of these things, which, in the words of Eliade, "answer a deep need of Western man." Yet we can only speak of these things from behind a mask.

In our language the word "mask" has a connotation of deception. But Nietzsche, the nineteenth-century German philosopher, observed, "Everything profound loves the

mask,"[7] to which the theologian Dietrich Bonhoeffer re-
marked one hundred years later, "Yet this mask is not a dis-
guise; it is not intended to deceive the other man, but it is a
necessary sign of the actual situation of disunion."[8] And then
Nietzsche again: "We no longer believe that truth remains
truth when it is unveiled . . . the shame with which Nature
has concealed herself behind riddles and enigmas should be
held in higher esteem."[9]

What does all this mean? It means that the expression "the
naked truth" is a contradiction in terms. It means that truth
is not naked but veiled, withdrawn, masked; it means that
the entrance to the Temple of Truth is a back entrance that
we can reach only by indirection when the light is dim; it
means that in this life we can behold the truth only "through
a glass, darkly."

As Sallie TeSelle observes: "Difficult, strange, unfamiliar
matters must be approached with the utmost cunning, imagination, and indirection in order for them to be seen *at all*."
And she concludes, "There is no direct way to talk about
God."[10]

Alfred North Whitehead "was wont to say that if one has a
perfectly clear and distinct idea about human experience, one
should immediately see a red light of warning that one is getting away from the realities."[11] (A reminder that for every
problem there is at least one simple, clean, and wrong solution.) What Whitehead has said of human experience, in
general, applies with equal validity to religious experience.
As soon as we have concocted a theology—or, for that matter,
a religious way of life—that is simple, logical, obvious, and
leaves no questions unanswered (I am thinking of the Evan-
gelical movements and their success in our present-day society), we may no longer be dealing with religious realities.

[9]

Having come to this insight, we are confronted with a disturbing question. For, isn't it true that we who are liberals pride ourselves on bringing reason to religion, on subjecting orthodox beliefs—some would say orthodox superstitions—to the test of rational inquiry, scientific insight, and knowledge? Isn't it true that we have seen as our task to bring light into darkness, to cull history out of stories, truth out of fiction, the real out of the unreal? How then can we, whose spiritual forebears gallantly tore the masks off the faces of the impostors, admit that in this age we have to mask our own faces in order to speak of religious realities? The future of liberal religion may depend on the answer to this question.

I cannot give the answer, only some suggestions.

The shadow of which T. S. Eliot speaks darkened three beacons that guided the course of liberal religion in the nineteenth and early twentieth century: science, reason, and the belief in man's perfectibility.

Science, whose astounding findings promised to lead man to an ever greater understanding of the universe, has led to results that transcend our intellectual faculties. Physicists, I believe, would be the first to agree that, at its cutting edge, science is spinning its own myths and that scientists, not wholly unlike theologians, are now speaking in parables and metaphors.

Reason as it was defined in the eighteenth and nineteenth centuries seems not to have kept its radiant promise in the twentieth. These lines by e. e. cummings reflect our disenchantment with traditional reason:

> minds ignorant of stern miraculous
> this every truth—beware of heartless them
> (given the scalpel,they dissect a kiss;
> or,sold the reason,they undream a dream) [12]

Carl D. Schneider writes: "Contemporary society . . . knows how to value only disclosure, demythologizing, unmasking. [The undreaming of dreams.] This one-sided preoccupation needs to be redressed. Mystery is as central to religion as is revelation."[13]

Finally, the nineteenth-century liberal's belief in man's basic goodness and perfectibility has been shaken by the wars and horrors of this century, by Verdun, Auschwitz, and Hiroshima.

No wonder that we liberals are confused. For what are we to do when we can no longer place reliance in science and reason and in man's development "upward and onward forever"?

No wonder that we are looking here and yonder, mostly eastward, hungry to find substitutes for a heritage we feel has failed us.

However, it is not our heritage that has failed us. It is we who are in danger of failing our heritage, the Judeo-Christian heritage that belongs to us and to which we belong. We are in danger of failing it in two ways:

First, by clinging to an inflexible nineteenth-century post-Enlightenment interpretation of that heritage whose orthodoxy of optimism makes it as outmoded, as obsolete, as are the orthodoxies of gloom it opposes.

Second, by assuming that this heritage claims to represent the truth of religion when in reality it represents the story of that truth, the metaphor about that truth. That metaphor demonstrates in history what is beyond history. It speaks to us in terms we know about things we do not know. It uses words for things that cannot be expressed in words, concepts for things that are inconceivable, images for things that are unimaginable. It addresses the truth by suggesting it and pointing to it, by evoking it and implying it. Yet this metaphor is not that truth and should never be confused with it.

I believe that this metaphor is our spiritual home.

I believe that we should put on our masks, as did Mr. Zuss and Nickles in *J.B.*, and play our part in it, having faith that in doing so we may, once in a while, experience the wonder of hearing that Distant Voice, guiding, consoling, comforting.

2

The Real and the True

In the beginning God created the heaven and the earth.

And the earth was without form, and void; and darkness was upon the face of the deep. And the Spirit of God moved upon the face of the waters.

And God said, Let there be light: and there was light.

GENESIS 1:1–5

"This is a fairy tale," protested the Orphan. . . .

"Of course it is a fairy tale," said the scientists, "but so is the world and so is life. That is what makes it true. . . ."

LOREN EISELEY, *The Cosmic Orphan*[1]

A great-aunt of mine was an old lady when I was still a pre-teenager, but I remember her well: an impressive Victorian figure with a lot of white hair and a friendly, ruddy face. I remember her for her kindness, but especially for a question she would invariably ask whenever anybody told her a story, an incident that had happened, or even a joke. After having listened carefully, the dear lady would inquire, "And is that a true story?" One day, in a mischievous mood, I told her some very unlikely tale, for the sole purpose of provoking that question once again, and, sure enough, after having listened carefully, she asked: "And is that a true story?" This time for some reason her question puzzled me, for while the story was not a likely one it might have been true; it was within the realm of the possible; it was not wholly absurd. I remember that I asked her, "How do you mean is it a true story?," and that she answered with great dignity and conviction: "A true story is a story that really happened." Her answer left me puzzled, for to a child the real and the true are not necessarily the same. Much later I realized that the old lady's answer touched upon vital theological questions: Has Jesus really lived? Was he really crucified? And resurrected? Are these true stories that really happened?

Around the year 200, the Roman theologian Tertullian wrote words that were to become famous: "God's son was crucified—that is no shame, because it is a shame; and God's son has died—that is likely because it is unthinkable; and having been buried he was resurrected—that is certain because it is impossible.[2]

The logic of the illogical did not die with Tertullian. The Middle Ages, in their buoyancy and love of contrast, never grew tired of repeating that the worldly illogical was the spiritual logical, that the worldly exception was the spiritual rule, that the worldly untruth was the spiritual truth. It was summed up in the ancient motto *credo quia absurdum,* "I believe (it) because it is absurd." It sounds preposterous but it can be rationalized. Colorless light that falls through a prism is broken into the spectrum of colors. Similarly, truth is broken when it shines through the prism of the world into the absurdity of worldly reality.

Children move with ease between truth, the way things are, and reality, the way things appear to be.

Take the story of Goldilocks and the Three Bears. Suppose you read it to a four-year-old and when you come to the scene in which great big papa bear says in a great big voice, "Somebody's been tasting my porridge," you say to the child: "At this point, according to the story, papa bear says something, but you know that bears cannot talk." Don't be surprised if the child says: "That is not true." For to the child, the truth is that papa bear does talk, and the fact that real bears do not talk does not weaken that truth. Children do not live in the reality of the world but in the truth of the story, the story in which animals can talk, in which flowers turn out to be bewitched princesses, and in which the child's kinship to all living things is much more truthfully expressed than in the reality of Charles Darwin's *Origin of Species.* For truth goes so far beyond the real that it can be conveyed only in the myth, the metaphor, the parable, and not in the reality it transcends; it is contained in the story about something, not in that thing itself.

One evening, many years ago, when I said good night to my youngest daughter, who was then five years old, she asked me the question that all children ask sooner or later: "Where was I before I was born?" This question does not refer to their prenatal earthly life; it is the ultimate question: "What is a human being, where do we come from?" I said: "Before you were born, you were with God; you were one of his littlest angels." The answer seemed to satisfy her. It satisfied me, too, and had my great-aunt asked me whether I had told my little girl a "true story," I would have been inclined to say: "Yes, that story was true, though it did not deal with reality." For the figurative and the symbolic, the parable and the meta- phor, are not the paraphrase of the real but the truth of the real. The real is within our grasp, but the truth is beyond it, and it is man's purpose to reach beyond his grasp, beyond what he can understand, smell, touch, see, define; to look over the edge of existence into the eternal mysteries of birth and death and love. And out of looking on these mysteries, out of meditating on these mysteries, religion is born. Truth is the continuation of reality into the beyond, and belief is the continuation of knowledge into the beyond. Or maybe the same thing can be better expressed by turning it around, by saying that knowledge is the worldly form of belief, and reality the worldly form of truth. Reality is of this world and is temporary. Truth is of the beyond and is eternal. In science we pursue the real; in religion, the true.

Thus defined, there is no conflict between science and religion, because they belong to different realms: science to the realm of the real, the material, the world; religion to the realm of the true, the unseen, the beyond. Scientists seek to express themselves in the realistic language of measures and figures, while prophets use the poetic language of myth and symbols. In science the lecture is used for verbal communication; in religion, the sermon. A lecture conveys information in terms that must be taken literally. Sermons do not convey information; they use symbolic language that points beyond itself and must not be taken literally. Thus language is used in different ways depending on whether it serves a scientific or a religious purpose. Of late these ways tend to merge in the realm of mystery as scientists on the frontier find that, in the words of P. W. Bridgman, "the structure of nature may eventually be such that our processes of thought do not correspond to it sufficiently to permit us to think about it at all. . . . The world fades out and eludes us. . . . We have reached the limit of the vision of the great pioneers of science, the vision, namely, that we live in a sympathetic world in that it is comprehensible to our minds."

As a result, scientists, too, can communicate certain insights only in symbolic terms.

There is a startling similarity between the most ancient tale of the true and the most modern insight into the real.

They agree that our universe has not always existed, that it has not run for endless time, but that the whole thing had a very definite beginning, that it began, so to say, from one day to the other. The Bible clearly states that there was a "beginning." The latest findings of astrophysics place the beginning at a point some ten billion years ago. There is no contradiction between Bible and science unless we break that timelessness—that "beyond" character—of the Bible, as the Irish bishop James Ussher did in 1654 when he declared that the beginning of which the Bible speaks, the creation of heaven and earth, took place in the year 4004 B.C. (at 9:00 A.M. on October 26, to be exact). Then the true is drawn from the realm of the beyond into the realm of the real. There its spell is broken and it becomes ridiculous.

Consider the serpent, the image of temptation that stands at the beginning of time. Was the serpent "real" or "only a symbol"? As a symbol, nobody can object to the serpent. But when the question arises whether the serpent has really spoken—I remember that in my youth Dominee Geelkerken, in the Netherlands, was expelled from the Reformed Church for the heresy of having doubted that the serpent had spoken with an audible voice—then the beyond is brought into the realm of the real and disintegrates.

Take the resurrection. In the Bible, the resurrection is used to suggest the immortality of the spirit, its awakening to new life on the other side of death, its leap into a world of brighter light and more perfect joy. But what did the early theologians do to this vision of spiritual life beyond death? They brought reality to it and transmuted the vision of spiritual immortality into the dogma of the physical resurrection. Once again, the submission of the true to the terms of the real resulted in something neither real nor true. Paul Tillich wrote: "The first step towards the non-religion of the Western world was made by religion itself. When it defended its great symbols not as symbols but as literal stories it had already lost the battle."[3] The real can destroy the true.

How real is the real? Up to the beginning of this century, this question would have been considered a philosophical question. From Euclid to Newton there seemed to be a world of the real, the measurable, the law-bound, the eternally stable. But since the advent of nuclear physics, that world has been superseded by a world the "reality" of which has become questionable. As Robert Oppenheimer states:

To the irritation of many, the assertions of science tend to keep away from the use of words like "real" and "ultimate." . . .

To what appeared to be the simplest questions, we will tend to give either no answer or an answer which will at first sight be reminiscent more of a strange catechism than of the straightforward affirmatives of physical science. If we ask, for instance, whether the position of the electron remains the same, we must say "no"; if we ask whether the electron's position changes with time, we must say "no"; if we ask whether the electron is at rest, we must say "no"; if we ask whether it is in motion, we must say "no."

And he rightly adds that such answers "are not familiar answers for the tradition of seventeenth and eighteenth-century science."[4]

Indeed, we have a right to ask how real the real turns out to be in the end. With regard to its relationship to the true, Oppenheimer says:

These two ways of thinking, the way of time and history and the way of eternity and of timelessness, are both part of man's effort to comprehend the world in which he lives. Neither is comprehended in the other nor reducible to it. They are, as we have learned to say in physics, complementary views, each supplementing the other, neither telling the whole story.[5]

That is why all efforts to define Jesus in historical terms are bound to fail. Albert Schweitzer, who made this effort, admitted the hopelessness of the task with the words: "The abiding and eternal in Jesus is absolutely independent of historical knowledge and can only be understood by contact with His spirit which is still at work in the world. In proportion as we have the Spirit of Jesus we have the true knowledge of Jesus."[6]

History is the record of the things that really happened, but the truth cannot be found in history. History can point to the truth but it cannot contain that truth. The truth can be contained only in the story, the story that begins with the words "In a faraway land" or "A long, long time ago" or "Once upon a time," and especially in the greatest story of them all, the story that opens with the words: "In the beginning God created the heaven and the earth. And the earth was without form, and void; and darkness was upon the face of the deep. And the Spirit of God moved upon the face of the waters. And God said, Let there be light: and there was light. . . ."

3

The Cosmic and the Cosmetic

For the Lord seeth not as man seeth; for man looketh on the
outward appearance, but the Lord looketh on the heart.

I SAMUEL 16:7

Woe unto you, scribes and Pharisees, hypocrites! for ye are
like unto whited sepulchres, which indeed appear beautiful
outward, but are within full of dead men's bones, and of all
uncleanness.

MATTHEW 23:27

The cosmic—according to the encyclopedia—is that which is
or pertains to the cosmos. The cosmos is the universe seen as
an orderly system. The cosmetic, according to the same
source, serves to beautify, to impart or improve beauty. The
cosmic is God-given. The cosmetic is man-made.

If one morning I look in the mirror and see that I have a
pimple on my nose, I witness a cosmic event. The pimple is
God-given. I am confronted with it, as I am confronted with
the cosmic order. If I apply to that pimple a cosmetic lotion
or ointment, I camouflage its ugliness. But underneath the
ointment the pimple is still there. I am not cured. I appear
cured. The cosmetic deals with appearance, the cosmic with
reality.

Does man's interference with the cosmic always have a
cosmetic character? Certainly not.

Take the story of the young minister and the old farmer.

One of the first projects the young minister undertook when he came to town was to get old Farmer Jones to come to church. For several Sunday afternoons in a row he drove up to the farm to have a chat with the old man. He praised the crop, he admired the cattle, he marveled at the chicken houses, but Farmer Jones barely acknowledged his remarks. On his third or fourth visit the young minister delivered his message: "Don't you feel that the Lord has blessed you, Farmer Jones? Don't you want to go to church and worship and give thanks to him?" Whereupon the old farmer said: "Young man, everything you have admired around here is the result of thirty years of hard work. Before I came here, the Lord had had the place to himself for thousands of years, and you should have seen the mess it was when I took over."

Farmer Jones had created order where the Lord had left disorder. Not in appearance but in reality. Farmer Jones had played a cosmic, not a cosmetic, role.

Some of you may be familiar with the story of Prince Potemkin, the Russian statesman and favorite of the Empress Catherine II. When, in 1787, he organized Catherine's tour of the newly annexed Crimean province, so the story goes, he had sham villages built along the horizon to impress his sovereign with the prosperity her rule had brought to the new territory. The story may or may not be true. But it is a perfect example of a cosmetic act, because it dealt with appearance, with pretense; it camouflaged the country's poverty as the ointment camouflaged the pimple.

Our world, our sociocultural environment, suffers, it seems to me, from an overdose of the cosmetic. Appearance is substituted for substance—that which looks good for that which is good, that which seems to be for that which is—so much so that, at times, we have the nightmarish feeling of living in a make-believe world. But, in the long run, the make-believe is not credible. The fact that we are suspicious of what we see and hear, what we are shown and what we are told, creates what is called, in an overused expression, the 'credibility gap,' which, if allowed to widen further, may one day swallow up the social order as we know it.

I read a story about a family—father, mother, children—whose car, late in the afternoon, had a flat tire. Father pulled over to the side of the highway and began to change the tire. It was getting dark. It began to rain. The cars on the highway swished by in an unending stream. Father had trouble getting the wheel off. The situation became uncomfortable. Then the voice of the five-year-old boy was heard: "Daddy, let's switch to another channel." He was a true child of our age. Why suffer? Switch the channel! He was brought up on the television diet of quasi-realities, sham realities, cosmetic realities, interchangeable realities. He no longer recognized the inevitability of real reality.

There are many good programs on television, and I don't want to throw out the television set with the bath water of the bad programs. But what a bath water it is, what a massive volume of contrived irrelevancies: situation comedies portraying synthetic situations, hospital stories misinforming people about hospitals, stories about courts of law that are not courts of law, about love that is not love, about people who don't talk or act like people! There is little truth in it.

The advertising industry has for years made its contribution to confusing people's sense of reality. Day in, day out, we hear infantile voices praise infallible cleansers; we are told of teeth without cavities, bodies without odor, stomachs that stop burning, colds that disappear, drugs more doctors prescribe and which are therefore better than other drugs fewer doctors prescribe, things composed of five ingredients that are therefore superior to things composed of fewer than five ingredients; we are shown cars that come in many models and models that come in many cars, animals that act like people and people that act like animals. Indeed, the advertising industry has handsomely contributed to the cosmetic pollution of our world.

Cosmetics have not left our language unaffected. I quote from an article by Grace Hechinger:

There are no prisons in a well-ordered society. Even Attica, at the height of the battle during which more than 40 men died, was meticulously referred to as a "correctional facility." . . . A headline on the front page of The New York Times announced recently: "Word 'Poverty' Faces U.S. Ban." . . . The U.S. Census has already . . . replaced "poverty" with "low income level." . . . Poor children have disappeared, if not from the slums, then at least from the language. First, they became "deprived," then "disadvantaged" and finally "culturally disadvantaged" as though they lacked nothing more serious than a free pass to Lincoln Center. . . . The neutral term "exceptional" is now applied equally to children of extraordinary intelligence and to the retarded and handicapped. No up-to-date pedagogue would call a boy lazy. He is an underachiever. . . . America has rid itself of old people by renaming them "senior citizens." . . . Department stores protect the sensitivities of their employees by referring not to theft or pilferage, but rather to "inventory leakage."[1]

Some years after these words were written, a flurry of indignation was aroused in the business community when a Harvard Business School professor was accused of having characterized lying as a commendable business practice. Only he did not call it "lying"; he called it "strategic misrepresentation."

The ultimate in cosmetic cover-up was William Calley's account of "wasting"—that is, killing—civilians during the war in Vietnam. "It makes murder seem painless," writes Grace Hechinger, "like wasting unwanted food." An older generation, however, may detect in William Calley's frivolous words an ominous echo of the term "final solution," with which the Nazis tried to cover up their murder of six million Jews. To these word-perverting whitewashers applies Jesus's castigation:

Woe to you . . . hypocrites! for you cleanse the outside of the cup and of the plate, but inside they are full of extortion and rapacity. . . .

Woe to you . . . hypocrites! for you are like whitewashed tombs, which outwardly appear beautiful, but within they are full of dead men's bones and all uncleanness. . . .

You serpents, you brood of vipers, how are you to escape being sentenced to hell?

And then there is the smile. Ah . . . the smile! You may think that people smile because something pleases them. Not so. Once this may have been true, but in our day the smile has become one of the most widely used cover-up mechanisms, hiding a wide spectrum of emotions, ranging from the subservient fearfulness of the ambitious young vice president who wants to please, to the desperate eagerness of the salesman who wants to sell. James Reston refers to the "official smile" as the "current fashion among world leaders." "There is . . . an aspect of unreality about all this," he says, "even an element of fraud . . . it is a good holding operation making things look good . . . but meanwhile the reality is hidden."[2]

Michael Novak's observation that "the airline hostess is

paid to smile in order to keep the impersonality of the mechanism from terrifying humans to death"[3] points to the functional as against the emotional nature of the contemporary smile. Most of the smiles that are smiled today have a function. They are mechanical facial expressions that do not correspond to a mood but are worn for cosmetic purposes, for pretending that all is well in a world in which many things are far from being well. "Things fall apart. There's nothing you can do. Let a smile be your umbrella," admonishes Jim Hougan.[4]

A certain degree of the cosmetic is needed if a civilization is to be civilized, but an overdose threatens its very existence because it estranges man from his environment. We experience this estrangement as our "identity crisis." Who am I? What kind of a person am I? But I submit that the source of that crisis may lie not with the individual but with the environment. What kind of an environment is this? What kind of a world is this? And from this question the next one is derived: How do I come to grips with or, possibly, how can I avoid coming to grips with this world, its complexity, its artificiality, its impersonality, its lack of veracity, its irreality?

The search for an answer to this question has set off a frantic quest for the cosmic by millions of people who hope that in some simple technique they may find that which is ever valid, ever real, ever true. It may not be by chance that in the jargon of one of the subcultures representing this search the highest praise was expressed with the words: "It's real, man!" There is this hunger for the real in a world in which so much is unreal.

"REAL WORLD," a young girl wrote to her father. "Our world, not yours. The world of everything, dream dance escape thought and blood."[5] This was in the early sixties.

Drugs had become part of the scene. The word "scene," in the jargon of the movement, signified "the whole of a setting and the action occurring within it."[6] The analogy to "the scene of a play with props, staging, actors and script"[7] makes the word sound strange in the mouths of those who were antipretense, anticosmetic, and dedicated to the search for the "real." A similar contradiction may be detected in the words with which the girl equates the "real world" with "dream dance escape thought and blood."

It was all part of the vocabulary of what one might call the subculture of the rude, the crude, and the nude. The rude (do away with all appearances of civilized behavior), the crude (tell it like it is, even—and maybe preferably—if it takes a sequence of four-letter words), the nude (let's uncover what the established culture has covered up). The motivating anxieties can be gleaned from the title of Jane Howard's report on the encounter movement, *Please Touch,* and its paperback promotion line: "Feel me, See me, Know me."[8]

Please touch because I am out of touch; feel me, for I've lost the feel of things; see me, for I'm dropping out of sight; know me, for I no longer know myself.

Many of us have participated in one or the other form of the human-potential movement: T groups, sensitivity groups, encounter groups, greater awareness—or expanded consciousness—training, EST. These techniques entered the mainstream of American middle-class life in the middle sixties. They became part of "a counterculture which rejected technocracy and instead embraced such values as mystical holism, trust in the intuition and the emotions, the person as of supreme worth, honesty and authenticity in self-expression, a personalist sense of community and a unification of politics with life-style."[9]

There was a "longing for a sense of genuine supportive community" with other like-minded human beings in order to overcome the pervasive feeling of "loneliness, anxiety, isolation, fragmentation." And a "hunger to be received just as I am," *i.e.,* without cosmetics, cover-up, or make-believe, "to be physically held and loved, to know oneself as received and affirmed by a stable group of significant others."[10]

This hunger "to be received just as I am," "to be physically held and loved . . . received and affirmed by . . . significant others" seems to me very much like the hunger of the infant; it is an infantile hunger, not the hunger of a mature, adult person.

Still, there is no question about the existence of this hunger and its appeasement—to a degree—by the more serious forms of this contemporary search for the cosmic. But in certain, more extreme, forms this search is as far removed from appeasing this hunger as is the indulgence in the cosmetic.

Thus, at a time when some churches benefit from the unexpected bonanza of the Jesus-freak movement (certainly a cosmic-searching movement, though a rather primitive one), we witness a renaissance of Satanism, the worship of the Fallen Angel, the Power of Evil. This worship takes many forms, from the medieval "black mass," an obscene persiflage of the church's most solemn sacrament, to the defilement of man's most prodigious cultural achievements, and the denial of his deepest insights.

The startling success of movies like *Rosemary's Baby* and *The Exorcist* bears out the fascination the Satanic holds for millions of Americans, as do numerous magazine articles like *Playboy's*, "The Devil and the Flesh," subtitled "A pictorial excursion into the occult—the dark, sensuous underworld ruled by lucifer and eros."[11]

The anticultural search for the cosmic and the cultural celebration of the cosmetic seem to me two sides of one and the same coin. The question is whether that coin is real or sham, because, in the end, the one side will be as real or as sham as the other side. I believe the coin is sham. If this is so, where does that leave us as individuals? It leaves us on a narrow ledge between the abyss of cosmetic make-belief and the abyss of cosmic belief-making, the ledge of spiritual truth between the two chasms of spiritual untruth.

We liberals often wonder what our religion is all about. Maybe it consists, at least in part, of the effort to widen that ledge by trying to distinguish the cosmic from the cosmetic, the true from the untrue.

"Remove from me the way of lying, and grant me thy law graciously," says the psalmist. "I have chosen the way of truth." That way of truth leads out of the cosmetic and quasi-cosmic worlds of trivial artificialities that will not endure into the cosmic mystery that speaks to us of things eternal.

4

❧

The Hedgehog and the Fox

It is no use trying to reconcile the multitude of egos that compose me.

HELEN KELLER, *Midstream*[1]

Observing my own conversational patterns on any given day, I note that I assume at least seven voices (seven: ancient number for the unlimited). I am strong, weak; helpless, infallible; dictator, slave; gentle one, angel of doom; Bogart, Mitty. With various others, in various situations, in various roles: how many different selves.

MICHAEL NOVAK, *Ascent of the Mountain, Flight of the Dove*[2]

"There is a line among the fragments of the Greek poet Archilochus which says: 'The fox knows many things, but the hedgehog knows one big thing.' " With this sentence the British scholar Isaiah Berlin opens his essay on Tolstoy's view on history.

Archilochus's dark words, says Berlin, "may mean no more than that the fox, for all his cunning, is defeated by the hedgehog's one defence. But," he muses, "taken figuratively, the words can be made to yield a sense in which they mark one of the deepest differences which divide writers and thinkers, and, it may be, human beings in general."

For there exists a great chasm between those, on one side, who relate everything to a single central vision, one system . . . in terms of which they understand, think and feel . . . and, on the other side, those who pursue many ends, often unrelated and even contradictory, connected, if at all, only in some *de facto* way . . . related by no moral or aesthetic principle; these last lead lives . . . that are centrifugal rather than centripetal, their thought is scattered or diffused, moving on many levels . . . without . . . seeking to fit them into . . . any one unchanging, all-embracing . . . inner vision.[3]

In thinking about Berlin's description of these two personalities, the first one obviously belonging to the hedgehogs and the second one to the foxes, it occurred to me that we modern Westerners, or at least the vast majority of us, are foxes; we are foxes who want desperately to be hedgehogs.

There was a time when Western man was a hedgehog. Medieval men and women did indeed relate everything to a single central vision; their life experience was governed by a single organizing principle that encompassed birth and death, sorrow and gladness, suffering and joy. All human experience was related to the ultimate mystery of Christ's birth, death, and resurrection. It was as if Meister Eckhart's supplication had been granted: "We beseech Thee, Lord God, to help us escape from the life that is divided into the life that is united." It was as if Thomas à Kempis's prayerful words had been heard:

Blessed are the single-hearted. . . .
He to whom all things are one, and who draweth all things to one, and seeth all things in one, can be steadfast in heart. . . .
A pure, sincere and stable spirit is not distracted in a multitude of works. . . .
O God, who art the truth, make me one with Thee. . . .
I am weary . . . to read and hear many things: in Thee is all that I desire and long for.[4]

Thomas did not want to be a fox, for the fox reads and hears and knows many things. We are the foxes; we know many things.

The ceaseless development from knowledge of one thing to knowledge of many things transformed medieval simplicity into modern complexity. In 1906 Henry Brooks Adams wrote, "The movement from unity into multiplicity, between 1200 and 1900, was unbroken in sequence, and rapid in acceleration. Prolonged one generation longer, it would require a new social mind."[5]

One of the events that set off the movement to multiplicity was the decentralization of the universe that resulted from Galileo's moving its center away from the earth to the sun. Galileo's troubles with the Catholic church, which led to his trial by the Inquisition in 1633, marked the beginning of the rupture between science and faith. Arthur Koestler says that the conflict could have been avoided. He feels that it was not Galileo's view of the universe that led to his trial for heresy, but the fact that he was a pugnacious troublemaker.[6] It is true that the vision of a sun-centered universe did not originate with Galileo, but with a timid canon in a cathedral town on the Baltic by the name of Nicholas Koppernigk, or Copernicus, some hundred years before Galileo's trial. One might indeed ask why did the church let Copernicus be and attack Galileo a hundred years later for propagating the Copernican view? The answer may be that Galileo was spreading the word. He shouted from the roof tops as truth what the timid canon had whispered within the confines of his study as a hypothesis. Moreover, the church may have nourished the hope that the Copernican views would be superseded by more conventional ideas, as had happened once before. For the Greeks of the sixth century B.C. conceived of an earth that turned around the sun, which theory subsequently was displaced by Aristotle's teaching of a motionless earth. The church may have hoped that the Copernican view would be similarly displaced.

Galileo's advent must have shaken any such hope, forcing the church into action in what became an extended and losing battle against scientific progress. This battle, more than any other single factor, estranged Western men and women from their church.

The church's concern about Galileo's proclamation, however, may have gone beyond the mere defense of its vested interest in a Bible-based, earth-centered universe. Some of its leaders may have wondered about the impact a shift of the center of the universe would have on humanity. Some may have felt that what was scientifically true—that the earth is not the cosmic center—was spiritually not quite so true. Some may have feared that the loss of the earth as the center of the universe would, in the end, lead to a centerless universe inhabited by centerless individuals. Which is what happened. For contrary to medieval man, we no longer have one center of our being, but many coexisting and often competing and contradictory centers. Each of us represents a composite, a multiplicity, a pluralism of centers and selves; we are no longer single-hearted.

In the words of Pitirim Sorokin:

The individual has as many different social egos as there are different social groups and strata with which he is connected. These egos are as different from one another as the social groups and strata from which they spring. If some of these groups are antagonistic to each other, then the respective egos that represent these groups in the individual will also be antagonistic.

Thus, " (the) 'family self' of an individual contrasts both in mentality and action with his 'occupational self'; both these differ from his 'religious' and 'state-citizenship' selves."[7]

As e. e. cummings wrote:

> so many selves(so many fiends and gods
> each greedier than every)is a man
> (so easily one in another hides;
> yet man can, being all, escape from none).[8]

Indeed, we are "divided within ourselves. The manifoldness of the world bewilders our minds."[9]

The manifoldness of the world. We know so many things that our minds are bewildered. None of us can know them all. This is what makes our age different from earlier ones. For the erudite Greek knew all there was to know in his world and so did the erudite Roman. To the early Christians knowledge of earthly things was suspect: "Whether there be knowledge, it shall vanish away," Paul writes to the church in Corinth and he admonishes the Ephesians "to know the love of Christ, which passeth knowledge." Thomas à Kempis seems to echo these words thirteen hundred years later: "Cease from an inordinate desire of knowing, for therein is found much distraction and deceit."[10] Christ, and his church, was the "one big thing," the only thing worth knowing.

The Renaissance and the centrifugal forces it set loose opened the way for the astounding ascendency of knowledge that culminated in the modern scientific revolution. Still, for many hundreds of years all knowledge could be encompassed by a single human intellect. Though men and women began to know many things, some individuals knew all these many things. The last of these individuals were the Encyclopedists in France, Diderot and his circle of friends, Montesquieu, Voltaire, Rousseau. Since the 1750s, you might say science has run amuck. Today we know so many things that none of us can know more than a small fraction of all that is known. This realization can be profoundly unsettling.

Haven't you at times felt desperate when you looked around a bookstore? There they lie, books by the thousands, covering subjects ranging from studies of the marital customs among the Hittites to the latest nonobjective poetry of the French existentialist avant-garde and the most recent theories of our astrophysicists, an overpowering multiplicity of which we know only one thing: nobody can read all this; life is too short even to cover the titles of all that has been written. Robert Oppenheimer says: "We are . . . an ignorant lot . . . of what is available in knowledge of fact, whether of science or of history, only the smallest part is in any one man's knowing."[11]

Is it any wonder that we feel perplexed and insecure? Is it any wonder that in our frustration we often experience existence as meaningless and empty?

These feelings, far from having been "invented" by modern existentialists though often attributed to them, were described toward the end of the nineteenth century by Gustave Flaubert:

Beneath us the earth is trembling. Where can we place our fulcrum, even admitting that we possess the lever? The thing we all lack is not style, nor that dexterity of finger . . . known as talent. We have a large orchestra, a rich palette, a variety of resources. We know many more tricks and dodges, probably, than were ever known before. No; what we lack is the intrinsic principle, the soul of the thing, the very idea of the subject. We take notes, we make journeys: emptiness! Emptiness! We become scholars, archaeologists, historians, doctors, cobblers, connoisseurs. What good is all that? Where is the heart, the verve, the sap?[12]

Goethe's genius made him press the question about the "one big thing" even earlier, when Faust, who had studied "Philosophy and Jurisprudence, Medicine and even, Alas! Theology," sells his soul to the devil

> So that I may perceive whatever holds
> The world together in its inmost folds.[13]

What is it that holds the world together? What is it? We who know so many things want to know that one big thing. We the foxes want to have the knowledge of the hedgehog.

It cannot be. There is no answer to this question—not for us. Not for us, that is, if we are honest, if we want to remain open-minded and free. Not for us who know so many things unless in our bewilderment we pretend not to know the things we do know. Unless we turn our back on that vast accumulation of knowledge and insight that forms our culture and in so doing narrow our perception to a single idea offered by the leader of some sectarian movement, a guru or a Führer. In the twenties, Pirandello wrote: "Don't you see what they are after? They all want the truth—a truth that is: something specific, something concrete! They don't care what it is. All they want is something categorical, something that speaks plainly!"[14]

Let us call this state of mind the state of narrowed perception. Only this state of narrowed perception can explain how in the heart of Europe, in one of the best-educated countries on earth, tens of millions could be made to believe that there was something like an Aryan race, the purity of which was going to save the world. Only this state of narrowed perception can explain how otherwise perfectly normal people can believe that all will be well if only we can get rid of the Catholic church or the Freemasons or the Jews or, for that matter, of the wealthy or the poor, the politicians or the prostitutes. How uncompromising they are: if black children enter their all-white schools, if Jews are admitted to their country clubs, if homosexuals are allowed in positions of authority, their world will come to an end. Their sham world of certainty, eked out of the real world of uncertainty; their simple world, cut out of the multiplicity and complexity of the real world. Yet their world is not that of the simple man but of the simpleton; it is not concerned with one big thing that can be contrasted to the world's many things, but with one miserable small thing to the defense and promotion of which they are totally committed.

The word "commitment" has a connotation of worthiness that may derive from its use in existentialist terminology as the English translation of Jean-Paul Sartre's term *engagement*. Walter Kaufmann warns us not to be misled by this recent upgrading which makes us feel that "the uncommitted life is not worth living" and that "any commitment is better than none."[15] That this last statement is patently untrue is self-evident. Yet it is supported by the realization that man's attainment of the greatest heights has generally been accompanied by the deepest kind of commitment. Jesus was deeply committed, as Socrates must have been and the Buddha before him. On the other hand, there is no doubt that the Nazis were deeply committed, as are many Communists. The nine hundred members of the People's Temple who perished in a mass suicide in Jonestown, Guyana in November 1978 were deeply committed, as are all pseudo-hedgehogs who, bewildered by the knowledge of many things, pick up one little thing in order to make it quasi-big. It would have been better if they had lived and died uncommitted.

They exemplify the quandary in which we find ourselves. For all of us know many things and we are inclined to think wistfully of the prophets and the saints who knew one big thing to which they devoted their lives, for which they were willing to die. They, it seems to us, knew what life was all about; we don't. They, or so it seems to us, were certain about ultimate things; we are floundering in doubt. They had time to think, while we have none; they could concentrate, while we are distracted; they could build on a solid, unified foundation, while we must build on the fragmented foundation of our multicentered, self-contradictory individuality. In our confusion we extend the number of our commitments to increasingly shallow and ephemeral causes, like the Chamber of Commerce, the Book-of-the-Month or the Record-of-the-Week clubs. In our bewilderment we run from one committee meeting to the other, from one social occasion to the other.

No wonder that psychiatrists' schedules are crowded, that the majority of hospital beds in this country are taken up by mental cases, that one out of every ten now-living Americans, so we are told, will at some time be hospitalized for a mental disturbance. The contradictions and uncertainties, the lack of direction, the absence of an agreed-upon set of values, the centerlessness of our lives leaves the individual, in the words of Sorokin, "an unhappy, tortured, self-contradictory creature, semi-insane and semi-criminal."[16]

No wonder that in our time uncounted millions of these unhappy, tortured creatures, "semi-insane and semi-criminal" sought escape from their fate by committing themselves to one single thing, like ever so many foxes trying to become hedgehogs. It didn't work. For the exclusiveness of their commitment was based on a lie: they denied knowledge of the many things out of fear that it would invalidate the one thing to which they had committed themselves. That denial made them into fanatics, not into hedgehogs.

The fox cannot become a hedgehog. The fox has to remain a fox. We have to recognize that our world is no longer unified and stable, as was that of medieval man, but pluralistic and dynamic, encompassing a multitude of kaleidoscopically changing insights, some of which appear contradictory, irreconcilable, and even mutually exclusive. Only if we accept this as historically given and unalterable can we hope to save ourselves from being or becoming the "unhappy, tortured" creatures described by Sorokin. For once we understand our predicament we can begin to make it bearable by disregarding futile insights and futile commitments and the knowledge of shallow things, and by devoting and committing ourselves solely to the knowledge of deeper things, however contradictory they may seem to be, however hard they may be to harmonize.

We must try to co-ordinate this knowledge and these commitments at the cost of much doubt and uncertainty, much groping and wavering, much trial and error and some compromise. And if we do so painstakingly and consistently, patiently and honestly, if we do not turn away from these things but think on them, then we may find that the manifoldness and multiplicity of our knowledge resolve themselves in the end into patterns of meaning. Then we may find that, in the end, the many things point to one big thing.

5

※

Continuity or Discontinuity

We are not only free organisms but parts of mankind that
has historically made itself with great inspirations and terrible conflicts. We cannot slough off the accumulation of it,
however burdensome, without becoming trivial and finally
servile.

PAUL GOODMAN, *New Reformation*[1]

. . . the absence of continuity in the coverage of events, as
today's crisis yields to a new and unrelated crisis tomorrow,
adds to the sense of historical discontinuity—the sense of
living in a world in which the past holds out no guidance to
the present and the future has become completely unpre-
dictable.

CHRISTOPHER LASCH, *The Culture of Narcissism*[2]

How continuous is continuous? An answer to this question
may be embedded in a story I heard when I was in grade
school. It described the vision of the universe held by a Hindu
tribe somewhere in India. Its members, so I was told, believed
that the earth and the sky above it rest on an elephant and
that the elephant stands on a turtle.

I remember that I was troubled by one particular aspect of
the story. It was not the role of the elephant. Maybe I had
already heard of Atlas, to whom the Greeks imparted a similar
role; if so, the analogy may have reassured me. Nor did I feel
disturbed by the idea of this obviously mythical elephant resting on an equally mythical turtle. What did bother me was

that nobody apparently had raised the question: And what does the turtle rest on? It was the absence of that question, let alone a satisfactory answer to it, that made me feel, as a young boy, that our Western way of thinking was superior to what I experienced to be the primitive ways of the East.

Today I appreciate the wisdom contained in the story. For I have learned that in the last analysis, whether it is in science or philosophy or theology, there is always that ultimate turtle on whom everything rests but who, in turn, rests on nothing.

Take our own religious beliefs, which are part of what is sometimes called the "Judeo-Christian tradition." The term has to be understood chronologically: Judaism preceded Christianity; the latter was derived from the former; the Christian church rests on Jewish foundations. The question of what Judaism rests on, the question about the older cultures from which Judaism is derived, traces of which can be found in the Old Testament, are questions we have delegated to specialized scholars. To most of us, the vision of Christianity resting on Judaism has a thoroughly acceptable finality.

A friend of mine who likes to travel where tourists do not go told me about an encounter he had with a tribe of natives somewhere in a hardly explored upstream region of Surinam. The natives overcame their mistrust when the traveler produced instant photographs of their leaders. Then something unexpected happened. The head of the tribe spoke up and told his people that they should follow the example of the white visitor. "Our wise men," he said, "take their wisdom with them in the grave but their wise men transmit their wisdom to their sons. They stand on each other's shoulders and that is why they can perform these miracles."

Out of his aboriginal primitivity he made a statement astonishingly similar to that made by Sir Isaac Newton: "If I have been able to see farther . . . it was because I stood on the shoulders of giants."[3] The same thought was expressed in our days by Lord Rutherford, one of the early atomic physicists, who said: "It is not in the nature of things . . . for any one man to make a sudden violent discovery; science goes step by step and every man depends on the work of his predecessors."[4]

It was William James who raised doubts about the absolute validity of this confident theory of cumulative knowledge when he said: "The greatest enemy of any one of our truths may be the rest of our truths."[5]

This statement certainly applies to our perceptions of religious truths. New perceptions replace older ones, causing, over long periods of time, deep conceptual changes in the way we perceive these truths. For our horizon is not a fixed one, but, as Michael Novak puts it, "a horizon-on-the-move."[6] Still, in spite of this open-ended, changing character of our perception, it would appear to me that the religious enterprise has over the ages revealed patterns of truth that survive these changes of perception and constitute man's cumulative heritage of timeless and abiding truths.

We of the liberal faith are in danger of losing this heritage of timeless truths because there are those among us who proclaim their independence from this heritage, who see it not as a treasure of timeless insights that enlighten us, but as a collection of obsolete superstitions that can only burden us.

The report of the Goals Committee commissioned by the board of the Unitarian Universalist Association and issued in the spring of 1967, spoke of a "new liberalism," which has "obvious connections with the past, having developed from

Protestant Christianity and the secular liberalism of the eighteenth century, [but] has moved so far from its origins that any simple historical analysis misses its present uniqueness." It draws the conclusion that "for its adequate expression we must build a distinctive religious institution which will develop more relevant skills, words and symbols."

I understand this to mean that we can no longer do justice to this "new liberalism" in historic terms. We can no longer express its essence in traditional terminology and symbols and images. History has become a burden, and we better start from scratch. I would like to refer to this view as the attitude of Discontinuity.

Many others have taken the opposite view, the attitude of Continuity. In the first number of *Zygon, Journal of Religion & Science,* the editors put it plainly:

On the question of whether to reform or to create a wholly new religion, we fancy we are scientifically informed enough to understand that we cannot lightly throw away ancient wisdom in any religious tradition. Man is not clever enough to produce a new language, religion, or any other cultural structure of long evolutionary history without starting from some model provided by prior cultural evolution. Even the especially rapidly evolving languages or concepts of the sciences and mathematics always arise out of the foundations laid by the cumulative experience of prior generations. Continuity of basic functions is as essential in the evolving patterns of cultural as in biological organization. Basic discontinuity is another way of spelling extinction.[7]

Robert Bellah observes: "In human affairs no beginning is absolutely new and every beginning takes meaning from some counterpoint of similarity to and difference from earlier events."[8] Newness anchors in oldness; the future has its roots in the past; the past is essential to the future. By forswearing the past, we may be foregoing the future.

Continuity or Discontinuity? This is the dilemma that faces the liberal movement. For our past is a Judeo-Christian past; the liberal movement has its roots in the Reformation; it originated in the liberal interpretation of the Bible. Yet today the study of the Bible has a low priority among us; many proclaim that the Bible is no longer "relevant" to present-day realities.

The problem whether the past is help or hindrance cuts across a much broader scene than that of any one denomination. It is central to the present conflict between the generations, in which the natural and desirable rebellion of the young against the established order threatens to become a rejection of that order.

Lewis Mumford alludes to this threat:

There is an . . . error . . . that now treacherously tempts the younger generation: the notion that in order to avoid the predictable calamities that the power complex is bringing about, one must destroy the whole fabric of historic civilization and begin all over again on an entirely fresh foundation. . . . As if human institutions could be improvised overnight![9]

The German author Günter Grass puts it this way: "The younger generation doesn't want to carry the burden of history. Sometimes it looks as though they are trying to step out of history, to start at zero. Then, after some time, they learn that it is not possible to start at zero."[10]

Many of our contemporaries would disagree with these statements because, as Harvey Cox observes, "Our period . . . is in revolt against the very idea of historical continuity itself." As an illustration, he quotes this passage from the writings of Lynn White, Jr.: "Our inherited intellectual processes, emotional attitudes and vocabulary are no longer of much use for analyzing and interpreting the spiritual revolution going on all around us." Cox notes that "it comes as a shock to realize that the man who uttered [these sentiments] is a distinguished scholar whose field is not cybernetics or psychedelics but medieval history." Professor White's conclusion: "The better we are educated, the more we are fitted to live in a world that no longer exists."[11]

Personally, I am a Continuity man, passionately so, and with deep conviction. I cannot see how we can neglect our religious heritage without becoming estranged from our cultural environment, thereby causing the ultimate dissolution of that culture and of the society it supports. For our culture is rooted in religion: a major part of Western music is religious music; a major part of Western painting and sculpture is religious painting and sculpture; most pre-Renaissance and Renaissance architecture is religious architecture, and the language we speak is permeated by biblical language, myth, legend, stories, and history.

Paul Tillich has called religion "the meaning-giving substance of culture" and culture "the totality of forms in which the basic concern of religion expresses itself."[12] There would be no St. Matthew Passion if Bach had not lived in the biblical tradition. The thought that one day people might be listening to the St. Matthew Passion or the B-Minor Mass without knowing what it is all about makes the cultural enterprise appear tragically absurd. The thought that one day people might look at van Eyck's "Adoration of the Lamb" and wonder whether it was meant to be an ad for a medieval brand of cattle feed fills one with horror.

That day may not be far off. In describing how the armies of summer tourists trudge dutifully behind the guides through Europe's cathedrals, an observer wrote: "Do I not perceive a look of non-recognition when the guides refer to Biblical events and the symbols of doctrine depicted in glass and stone? Do many of these vacationers herded through Chartres and Reims react to the advertisements of Christian tradition otherwise than they would to the dead religions of Stonehenge, Delphi and Thebes?"[13]

Harry Emerson Fosdick told of a sign he once saw in Maine. It said: "Be up-to-date. Buy your antiques here." This is not what I am saying. What I am saying is that the past is not an antique, that the past is not past, but that it lives in the present and will be part of the future.

Carl Scovel once said in a sermon: "Our past does live—it lives in our expectations of life, in how we treat the butcher and the banker; it lives in our songs and hopes, in our patterns of living." He raises and answers the question: Why do we study our past?

We study our past to understand ourselves—now—today. For we find ourselves in the lives of these strange and wonderful men and women who wander through the pages of the Bible, our church's heritage and the folklore of other faiths; some are bad, some are good; some are brave, some are cowards; some are pious, some are proud; some love God and some love themselves. But we learn from all of them, for we *are* all of them.

I agree. Even the Goals Committee of the Unitarian Universalist Association admitted that this small denomination is rooted in Protestant Christianity to which, some of us would argue, it still belongs today. In the past its role within Protestantism has been that of a dissenting minority that rejected the concept of the Trinity, the thesis of the inerrancy of the Bible, and that generally opposed orthodoxy. It has refused to subscribe to any dogma and has abstained from insisting on any creed lest it infringe upon the spiritual and intellectual freedom of its members. Historically, it has been the gadfly of the church, and its liberalizing and humanizing influence has at all times been far out of proportion to its small size. Only the Quakers can point to a similarly fortuitous disproportion.

We liberals were able to play this role because we expressed our disagreement with the established churches in a language that we shared. We voiced dissenting views with respect to matters in which we had a common interest. While the results of our, and their, search for truth may have been different, we searched for truth in the same areas and with respect to the same questions. Our relationship with them illustrated the validity of the French saying *Pour discuter il faut être d'accord*—freely translated: In order to disagree there must be an area of agreement. This area of agreement is slowly disappearing, oddly enough at a time when the development within the more orthodox churches would be conducive to a growth of that area of agreement were it only because of the shrinkage of the areas of disagreement. We liberals gave up at a time when our chances of having an impact were better than ever. We copped out at a time when we could have made our greatest contribution. We discontinued the dialogue at a time when it might have enriched and rewarded both sides more than ever before. Instead, we turned our back on the contemporary religious scene: we left the mainstream of contemporary religious life, and find ourselves, in the terms of Emerson's famous dictum, living in solitude after our own opinion. We are estranged from tradition, which Oppenheimer once called "the matrix which makes discovery possible."

Some liberal churches, as Donald Harrington has observed, risk becoming "all-accepting conglomerates of people affirming their right to believe whatever they want to, who exalt in the exhibition of their idiosyncrasies, who delight in the philosophy that 'anything goes' and 'everything is right.' "[14] Everything is right and anything goes except the things that are reminiscent of our religious tradition and origin, for on that point these ultraliberal groups are as orthodox as the blackest fundamentalists. Indeed, we have among us today a liberal orthodoxy that is as narrow and intolerant as any orthodox orthodoxy.

Harrington expresses the hope that we may rediscover the significance and enduring value of our religious past, which would mean "that many of the old words and myths and symbols will be seen in a new perspective and shine forth with a new significance as we discover their modern counterpart . . . words like God, covenant, law, pilgrimage, incarnation, salvation, perdition, atonement, virtue and sin. . . ."[15]

This vocabulary comes to us from the remote past. Its significance in the present would indeed have to be rediscovered because most liberals are no longer familiar with these words and have lost the sense of their deeper meaning. Some may feel that this is the price paid for having played the role of gadfly. If this were true, it would be a ruinous price.

I think I am on pretty safe grounds with a plea against theological illiteracy, disrespect for the past, and negligence of tradition, because I think that even those who opt for Discontinuity can validly do so only if they know what they are discontinuous with.

[47]

Earlier I confessed my personal commitment to Continuity. Although I dare not exclude the possibility of creative Discontinuity and concede that it might just be possible that our world can rest on nothing, I for one remain convinced that our world needs an elephant to rest on and that the elephant needs a turtle.

II

SUFFERING

6

⚜

Between the Silences

And they came with haste, and found Mary, and Joseph,
and the babe lying in a manger.

And when they had seen it, they made known abroad
the saying which was told them concerning this child.

And all they that heard it wondered at those things which
were told them by the shepherds.

But Mary kept all these things, and pondered them in her
heart.

LUKE 2:16–19

And when Herod saw Jesus, he was exceeding glad . . .
because he had heard many things of him; and he hoped to
have seen some miracle done by him.

Then he questioned with him in many words; but he
answered him nothing.

LUKE 23:8–9

Before some ultra-liberal congregations it takes courage
these days for the preacher to read from the Bible. It makes
the preacher suspect, if not outright unacceptable. Such is
the intransigence of some present-day liberals; such is the
intolerance of liberal neo-orthodoxy.

I begin to find this intolerance quite intolerable.

The "thou shalt not" attitude it signifies is, in itself, obviously unliberal and represents a rigidity that we used to
impute to more orthodox persuasions. But it goes beyond
that, for all of us risk being deprived of our religious and

cultural heritage by the prejudice of some who hold that the past is past and that contemporary needs can be met only by contemporary means. This troubles me because it is my deep conviction that contemporary religious concepts can be conceived and understood only within the perspective of an existing continuity of religious imagery and symbolism. In addition, religion needs an agreed-upon vocabulary: it needs language. There is a mutuality between language and feeling, between the ability to verbalize something and the ability to experience something emotionally. Arthur Foote once said in a sermon: "What we can not somehow put into words, we can not adequately feel. When we can not speak of God in ways that are meaningful and comfortable, we largely lose our capacity to open ourselves to the workings of his spirit."

We must regain the capacity to speak of things of the spirit. This means that we must among ourselves preserve and create religious terminology on the meaning of which there is at least a minimum degree of agreement lest we lose ourselves in an erratic maze of language.

We must train ourselves not only to use language but also to permit language to use us. We must train ourselves to listen to language, to its undertones and overtones, to its connotations, to its evocative and poetic qualities, through which language points beyond itself to the realm where indeed "words fail us" and where there is only silence.

Of two such silences the mystery of Christmas is made. The first is Mary's silence: "And all they that heard it wondered at those things which were told them by the shepherds. But Mary kept all these things, and pondered them in her heart." The other is the silence Jesus keeps when he stands accused before Herod, who "questioned with him in many words; but he answered him nothing." Between these two silences lies the life of him whose birth we commemorate in the Christmas season.

You may say that the second silence does not belong to Christmas but, rather, to Easter, that it is not part of the birth of the babe but part of the death of the man. However, Christmas was originally the festival of birth and death and rebirth. Long before the Christian era, this season was celebrated as the season of rebirth of the sun, which moves at this time through the winter solstice toward the lengthening of the days. The Christian celebration of the child's birth was superimposed on the pagan celebration of nature's rebirth; and in our symbols of Christmas we find the strands of both traditions. The turn of the seasons is celebrated by our bringing into our homes trees and holly and mistletoe, the exact meaning of which is obscure. Was it originally an effort to preserve life by giving it shelter? Or was it a way of paying tribute to life by beautifying the trees? Or maybe an inducement to bring forth fruit? Or was there possibly a subconscious desire to bring nature into the protective womb of the home pending its rebirth in the spring? Who is to say? We know only that the coming and going of the seasons in their eternal cycle form the background for the unique event of the child's birth.

That uniqueness is suggested by the tales of what happened during the night. For it is at night that wondrous things happen. It is in the stillness of the night that time empties itself into eternity, that the finite recognizes itself in the infinite.

> O Man! Take heed!
> What words from midnight's depth arise? . . .
> "The world is deep,
> And deeper than the day's surmise."[1]

These lines by Nietzsche are somehow related to the mood of Luke's story, as are Job's words: "He discovereth deep things out of darkness." Deep things, wondrous things. Mary pondered them in her heart in silence, the silence of the unutterable.

How different was Jesus's silence. It is mentioned in all three synoptic gospels. In Matthew and Mark it is Pilate whose questions he ignores. In Luke's gospel, it is Herod who, in haughty indifference to Jesus's plight and oblivious of his judicial duties, was "exceeding glad for he . . . hoped . . . to have seen some miracle done by him. Then he questioned with him in many words; but he answered him nothing." We see Herod before us, quasi-jovial, verbose, and vulgar, bent on satisfying his sensationalism by cajoling his victim into performing just one more miracle before being led away so that he, Herod, could tell his friends about it, back home. Jesus stood there and found it all unspeakable and kept silent: the silence of the unspeakable.

Between the silence of the unutterable and the silence of the unspeakable lies Jesus's life. Between them lies the life of each of us. All of us live between these two extremes. There is beauty in our lives, and love and tenderness; there is the mystery evoked by music, by the sea, and the stars, by the touch of the beloved, the laughter of a child. But then, there is the laughter of the soldier at Songmy who, in the words of Sergeant Michel Bernhardt, "laughed every time he pressed the trigger." ("He just couldn't stop. He thought it was funny, funny, funny.") [2] There are the purges and persecutions in Stalinist Russia, the Nazi death camps, the massacres in Indonesia and Biafra and other third world countries, the cattle prods and fire hoses of Sheriff Bull Connor, the deaths in Vietnam's tiger cages and South Africa's prison cells, the

[54]

endless triumphs of stupidity and vileness and senselessness the world over. We are reminded of the teaching of certain existentialists that all that is demanded of man, all that can be expected of man, is to endure the meaninglessness of life.

Mystery and meaninglessness, the unutterable and the unspeakable.

A little girl asked her father: "Why do we speak of the *good* Lord?" Whereupon the father said: "Some weeks ago you were suffering from measles, and then, the *good* Lord sent you full recovery." However, the little girl, far from being content, retorted: "Well; but, please, Daddy, do not forget: in the first place, he had sent me the measles."[3] That little girl had not even read the book of Job!

Another story comes to mind, the story of a little girl, four years old, and one of those old-fashioned gas water heaters. One day she was standing in the bathroom ready to climb into the tub when the heater exploded. The little girl ran out of the house without taking anything along to cover her nakedness and disappeared into the surrounding woods. When she was found many hours later, she expressed her unwillingness to return home with the words: "I do not want to go back to a house where things like that happen." Of course, in the end she did go home, for it was the only home she had.

We find ourselves in a similar situation. This is our world; it is the only world we have. As the little girl found out, there is no alternative. We have to face the unspeakable. We have to wrestle with the question of why we get the measles; we have, somehow, to accept the fact that water heaters will explode. That is why Christmas is not only about the birth of the babe and the things that happened on that night in which humankind may have dreamed its most visionary dream; but also about the death of the man and the vulgar scene before Herod in which a bunch of conspiring extremists exploited the haughty indifference of the local rulers in an orgy of profane meaninglessness. The meaningfulness of that wondrous night is, in the deepest sense, derived from the meaninglessness of that cruel day, and the meaninglessness of that day is overcome by the meaningfulness of that night. This is the significance of Christmas for both believers and nonbelievers.

Viktor Frankl wrote: "What is demanded of man is not, as some existential philosophers teach, to endure the meaninglessness of life; but rather to bear his incapacity to grasp its unconditional meaningfulness in rational terms. Logos [meaning] is deeper than logic."[4]

Frankl is a survivor of the Auschwitz extermination camp; in the death camp of Auschwitz he found the meaning of life.

All of us experience in our own lives both the mystery of the unutterable and the misery of the unspeakable. We find it desperately difficult to face that misery when it confronts us; we try to run away from it, as the little girl ran away when the water heater exploded, only to find, as she did, that in the end we have to face it.

At such times life appears unbearable to us and we become oblivious to its mystery and reproach life for denying us a fair deal. We begin to take it out on others by being self-righteous, or on ourselves by being self-destructive. Then we should remember him who remained silent when the unspeakable confronted him and with his silence gave meaning to the meaningless. In his silence the unutterable conquered the unspeakable.

He did not, however, remain silent when he saw others confronted with the unbearable. He spoke up and came to their rescue; he went out and healed the sick, comforted the sufferers, and encouraged the desperate. It was he who answered Cain's age-old question whether man is his brother's keeper, and he answered it in the affirmative. Most of us will speak up when we feel that injustice is done to us but remain mute when injustice is done to others. He spoke up against injustice done to others and remained mute about injustice done to him.

Some years ago people were startled by the story of those who looked out of their windows somewhere in Queens and saw Kitty Genovese murdered and they never made a move. Sometime later I read about a cabbie who refused to take a woman to the hospital, so that she had to give birth to her child in the street while none of the onlookers made the slightest attempt to assist her. In the Bronx, a man who fought off a holdup attempt for twenty minutes could not persuade any passer-by to summon a policeman to help him. "I begged them to call the police," he said. "I shouted 'these people tried to hold me up,' I said to them 'I'm Puerto Rican just like you,' but it was like talking to empty air, to the floor. They just walked faster away."[5]

How he would have castigated them.

On the other hand, it is not difficult to imagine how he would have encouraged the civil-rights workers and the Peace Corps men and women and so many of our young people who stand up for their convictions and cheerfully go to jail rather than compromise on their principles. He would have been with Martin Luther King, Jr., and the inner-city ministers and all those who are trying to come to grips with the problems of racial injustice and poverty and hunger and pollution in our own country and abroad.

Ours is a time of unspeakable evil but also of selfless efforts to remedy that evil. The despair of our days, which is great, has not left us without hope. That is why we can, as of old, celebrate the child's birth as a symbol of the birth in us and around us, of hope out of despair, meaning out of meaninglessness, and light out of darkness.

7

The Burden of Knowing

And Jesus answering said, A certain man went down from Jerusalem to Jericho, and fell among thieves, which stripped him of his raiment, and wounded him, and departed, leaving him half dead.

And by chance there came down a certain priest that way: and when he saw him, he passed by on the other side.

And likewise a Levite, when he was at the place, came and looked on him, and passed by on the other side.

But a certain Samaritan, as he journeyed, came where he was: and when he saw him, he had compassion on him.

And went to him, and bound up his wounds, pouring in oil and wine, and set him on his own beast, and brought him to an inn, and took care of him.

LUKE 10:30–34

I do not think there is a better-known story in the Bible than the parable of the good Samaritan. Only it is not the Samaritan's story alone; it is also that of the highway robbers and their victim, of the innkeeper, and especially of the Levite and the priest, who, when they saw from a distance that somebody was lying on the road detoured around him and passed by on the other side.

In the terminology of American Westerns, you might say the Samaritan was the "good guy" and the priest and the Levite the "bad guys." But then, it may not be quite that simple; the "bad guys" of the story really are the highway robbers. The priest and the Levite are not necessarily bad.

Maybe they just had no time. Maybe the priest was on his way to meet with a wealthy man who considered making an important gift for the poor in his congregation. He could not risk offending him by being late. Maybe the Levite was on his way to deliver a lecture on some theological subject in a nearby town. If he was late, he might be blamed for permitting himself to get entangled in some ludicrous situation with a dying tramp. It may well be that this was the reason for the behavior of the priest and the Levite: they did not want to get entangled; they felt that they could not afford to get involved. Being decent people who would not withhold assistance if they knew that it was needed, they preferred not to know. This, I think, was the reason they passed on the other side of the street, quickening their step, casting in passing a furtive glance at that man lying helpless on the road to Jericho, and then looking again ahead without turning around. They did not want to know what had happened; they did not want to know whether the man was dead or alive. They did not want to know.

The priest and the Levite were not "bad guys"; they were self-protective guys, as you are, as I am, as all of us are. We, too, prefer not to know. We, too, are inclined to avoid entanglements and pass by on the other side, minding what we call "our own business," which is sometimes very burdensome. We, too, avoid becoming involved with other people's suffering and anguish. Here is one of the paradoxes of our day: we, as no generation before us, are eager to collect information, facts, figures, data. We are hungry for knowledge, but we are fearful of knowing.

"I did not know." These are the magic words with which we absolve ourselves from our sins of omission, the homage selfishness pays to conscience.

With these words an entire nation tried to disavow its responsibility for the abominable and hideous crimes that for years on end were committed in its midst. The concentration camps? Sure, there were camps, but we did not know what was going on inside. Millions of people were tortured and murdered? Maybe, but we did not know. Besides, it was none of our business, and those war years were tough, for we had a lot of trouble of our own.

Does this mean that all those Germans were bad? No, it only means that they wanted to remain free from the anguish of the persecuted. They did not want "to be touched, contaminated, soiled, involved."[1] They wanted to remain aloof and mind their own business. They were filled with self-pity about their own troubles, which were small and petty compared to the desperate conditions of those suffering and martyred millions whose plight they ignored as the priest and the Levite ignored the man lying on the road to Jericho.

And what about us? Do we want to know what is happening around us, in our prisons, in our mental hospitals, a few blocks from where we live? The press reports regularly about subhuman conditions in homes for the aged, about overcrowded reform schools, inadequate prison facilities. We have the knowledge, but we do not want to know. If somebody were to come up to us and say, "Let me tell you about the conditions in the slums of New York's South Bronx, how they breed addiction and crime," wouldn't we be inclined to say, "You do not have to tell me; I know, I know, I know," meaning, "I do not want to know."

In the book of Ecclesiastes we read: "in much wisdom is much grief: and he that increaseth knowledge increaseth sorrow." In much wisdom is much grief. The root of the word is *wis,* the same as of the German word *wissen,* that is, to know.

Wisdom in this sense is knowledge or knowing. We find the same root in our words "wit" and "witness." If you have witnessed something, you know it. You have seen it with your own eyes. The archaic Greek verb *eido* (again from the same root) has two meanings: one, to see, the other, to know.

The priest and the Levite refused to see, to witness, to know. That is what, at least on one occasion, Adolf Eichmann refused to do. According to his taped testimony, he was once taken to a place where children were killed, and he said that he could not bear to look; he looked the other way. He could not bear to witness what was going on. Though he had been instrumental in organizing the hideous crime, he did not want to know.

Eichmann was not the only one in modern history to look the other way. Nor is the refusal to know limited to criminals. No less a gentleman than General Sir Douglas Haig, who sacrificed four hundred ten thousand British soldiers in the battle of the Somme in 1916, is reported by his son to have felt "that it was his duty to refrain from visiting the casualty clearing stations because these visits made him physically ill."[2]

These cases illustrate in a fearful way the modern paradox, the contradiction between our thirst for knowledge, for information, and our fear to assume the burden of knowing. We are afraid to know, for in much wisdom—that is, in much knowing—is much grief.

At the same time, these illustrations point to the deadly danger inherent in that paradox: if we cannot overcome our fear to know, if we are unwilling to assume the grief that goes with the "wisdom," the witnessing, then there is no limit to the crimes we may commit, then we lose our humanity and revert to the jungle from which we once emerged.

The sources of our humanity are consciousness and conscience. The etymology of these words is revealing: both are
composed of the Latin prefix *cum* (with or co) and the verb
scio, which means to know. My conscience, therefore, is my
co-knower. It is the still small voice within; it is a part of me
but at the same time apart from me. It is an alter ego with
whom I have an ongoing dialogue; it is my censor and guide,
my counselor and mentor. It observes me as if from the outside and speaks to me about what I am. This is the state of
human consciousness; to be conscious means that I know that
I am.

Rollo May praises man's consciousness of himself as the
source of his highest qualities: "It underlies his ability to
distinguish between 'I' and the world. . . . This capacity for
consciousness of ourselves gives us the ability to see ourselves
as others see us and to have empathy with others. . . . It
enables us to imagine ourselves in someone else's place, and
to ask how we would feel and what we would do if we were
this other person."[3]

Martin Buber marvels at man's awareness of the universe:
"Man is the being who knows his situation in the universe
. . . he knows the relation between the universe and himself. Thereby from out of the midst of the universe something that faces the universe has arisen."[4] But this awareness
is preceded by man's awareness of himself: out of the individual, something that faces that individual has arisen. That
is the individual's conscience.

Meanwhile, it is clear that these co-knowers, conscience
and consciousness, which elevate man out of his animal status,
are also the causes of much sorrow and anguish. We pay a
price for our emancipation from the limitations of the animal
world. For consciousness is the source of regret about a re-

membered past, fear of an unknown future, anxiety about the uncertainties of life, and horror at the certainty of death. No wonder that some balk at paying that price. No wonder that some have expressed a nostalgia for the innocence of the animal that is without consciousness or conscience. Walt Whitman was one of them:

> I think I could turn and live with animals, They
> are so placid and self-contain'd,
> I stand and look at them long and long.
>
> They do not sweat and whine about their condition,
> They do not lie awake in the dark and weep for
> their sins,
> They do not make me sick discussing their duty to God.
> Not one is dissatisfied, not one is demented
> with the mania of owning things,
> Not one kneels to another, nor to his kind that
> lived thousands of years ago,
> Not one is respectable or unhappy over the
> whole earth.[5]

This is Walt Whitman's indictment of consciousness and conscience, his prayer for return to the innocence of the animals, the lament of one who having accepted the burden of knowing had experienced its grief. His prayer for delivery stems from the depth of that grief.

We do not want to share that grief; we try to protect ourselves against it; we try to walk away from it, to pass on the other side.

I have begun to wonder whether our desire to avoid grief is the only reason why we do not want to know. Is it possible that our unwillingness to add to our knowledge results also from the fact that we already know so much?

I came across these lines in "Choruses from 'The Rock'" by T. S. Eliot:

> The endless cycle of idea and action,
> Endless invention, endless experiment,
> Brings knowledge of motion, but not of stillness;
> Knowledge of speech, but not of silence;
> Knowledge of words, and ignorance of the Word.
> All our knowledge brings us nearer to our ignorance,
> All our ignorance brings us nearer to death,
> But nearness to death no nearer to GOD.
> Where is the Life we have lost in living?
> Where is the wisdom we have lost in knowledge?
> Where is the knowledge we have lost in information?[6]

It has not always been this way. There was a time when men and women asked no questions except those to which the church gave the answer. Beyond that they had no desire for knowledge or information. They knew; medieval men and women were fully integrated in the mold of an all-encompassing, harmonious, static, religious system, completely reasonable within its basic assumptions, "surrounding the individual's life from birth to death, sanctifying and enclosing all its ordinary and extraordinary occasions in sacrament and ritual."[7]

The decline of religion that set in at the end of the Middle Ages and continues to our present day has meant more to man than a loss of certain beliefs that became untenable in the light of science. William Barrett says:

The loss of the Church was the loss of a whole system of symbols, images, dogmas, and rites which had the psychological validity of immediate experience, and within which hitherto the whole psychic life of Western man had been safely contained. In losing religion, man lost the concrete connection with a transcendent realm of being; he was set free to deal with this world in all its brute objectivity. But he was bound to feel homeless in such a world, which no longer answered the needs of his spirit. . . . To lose one's psychic container is to be cast adrift, to become a wanderer upon the face of the earth.[8]

To him applied the psalmist's outcry, "I am a stranger in the earth, hide not thy commandments from me," as well as A. E. Housman's lament

> I, a stranger and afraid
> In a world I never made.[9]

We are not the first generation to feel estranged from God and man. But we may be the last. We did not make this world, but we may *un*make it. For, if we continue to refuse to assume the burden of knowing, the process of dehumanization will continue until one day some man-made Univac or some Univac-made man will press the fatal button.

There is no way back to the old medieval certainty of knowing. We begin to realize that modern science will not lead us into a new certainty of knowing either.

A group of professors of science, mostly from the Massachusetts Institute of Technology, met for several days of conference one summer to discuss how science textbooks, for use with elementary and high-school children, should be rewritten in the light of modern scientific insights. One question was raised over and over during their deliberations: At how early an age dare we tell children that we are uncertain?

At about the same time, the British archaeologist Jacquetta Hawkes wrote: "I should like to insist that nearly all the really important questions, the things we ponder in our profoundest moments, have no answers."[10]

The myth of Medieval Religion is dead. The myth of
Scientific Religion is dying. We will die with it unless we
realize that our knowledge of the expanding universe will not
comfort one single crying child and that the scientific pro-
longation of man's life expectancy will not dispel the loneliness of one single aged man or woman. We will die unless
we succeed in converting our knowledge into knowing, unless
we take upon ourselves the burden of knowing and co-know-
ing, unless we overcome our fear of getting involved, unless
we give up passing by on the other side of the street. We have
to learn again that in minding our neighbor's business we
mind our own business and that we are our brother's and
sister's keeper.

Once, on an early spring day, I walked on the Biblical road
that leads from Jerusalem to Jericho. It was as I had always
imagined it: an old, dumb country road winding slowly
through the valley following the way of least resistance, avoiding the slopes of the surrounding hills the modern road cuts
through. I had always wanted to walk on that road, as if it
were the scene of a most important historical event and not
just the scene of a story. The reason may be that this story had
become history to me. Thus, the mythical enters into the
religious structures we build out of the history of the race. I
think this is what Michael Novak refers to when he says:
"Human acts, it may safely be asserted, have a base in myth;
there is no human act that is not an acting out of a story."[11]

There is something ultimate about this particular story.
For much will pass, much will change, much will be abro-
gated. But I am convinced that when the human race will
have spread into space, when truths we have never thought of
will have become evident, when undreamed-of insights will
have replaced our still-primitive concepts of the universe,

[67]

the ultimate deed will still be that of the Samaritan, the Samaritan who did not start an investigation, who did not begin a movement to abolish thievery, who did not go into the sociological or psychological question "what makes robbers rob," but who simply, on finding his brother in need, "had compassion on him . . . bound up his wounds . . . and brought him to an inn, and took care of him."

In the confusion and despair of our days we can still see the image of the Samaritan, and his features are those of the man of compassion, acquainted with grief. If there is to be a future, it will be his.

I have occasionally been asked to make suggestions for the curriculum taught to students at our theological schools. I have never felt qualified to make such suggestions. Today, however, I would say: Above all, speak to them of the Samaritan.

8

✠

The Willingness to Suffer

Early Christianity won the day in Rome because it told the
slave-woman, daughter of a slave, watching her slave child
dying in vain, as it had been born in vain, "Jesus . . .
died in agony . . . so that you should not have to face this
agony of yours alone."

ANDRÉ MALRAUX, *The Voices of Silence*[1]

The two promises we make to our patients are: one, we will
keep them free from pain; two, they will not die alone.

MICHAEL STOLPMAN[2]

Suffering is not fashionable these days. If you bring it up in
conversation, you make yourself suspect. Why discuss suffering in a society that is engaged in the pursuit of happiness?
Why not speak of confidence or courage, of peace of mind
and serenity of soul; why not speak of the fuller life, the
better life, of how to overcome sickness through faith and
poverty through initiative? Why not conform to the American cult of the ingratiating smile and the boyish grin that
spell self-assurance and success?

Many years ago a national picture magazine devoted an
issue to the Du Pont family of Wilmington, Delaware. It dis-
played a photograph of four generations named Irénée Du
Pont: the elderly grandfather, the middle-aged father, the
pre-teenage son, and, on the wall, the portrait of the great-
grandfather. Great-grandfather and great-grandson looked

[69]

serious, but the grandfather and the father, as behooves successful captains of industry, wore broad smiles, as if reassuring the readers that all was well with the Dupont firm and with the world at large. For underlying this cult of the stereotyped smile is the notion that the sad and the dismal, the causes of tragedy and pain, are mere accidental infringements upon a human condition that was meant to be, and, therefore, should be, happy and pleasant.

But this is not the way it is. Suffering is not miscarried joy or happiness gone wrong. Suffering is implicit in human life. Its origin can be traced to the seductive words the snake spoke to Eve: "In the days ye eat thereof, then your eyes shall be opened," that is, you shall have vision. This vision enables us to visualize realities other than the reality of the moment—historical ones from the past, potential ones in the present, imagined ones in the future. And out of the comparison of what is with what has been, what could be, and what may be come both our suffering and our striving.

To some the Paradise story signifies the fall of man. To others it signifies his birth. Some see in God's words to Eve, "I will greatly multiply thy sorrow," and to Adam, "In sorrow shalt thou eat of it all the days of thy life," a curse, a punishment for disobedience. To others they represent the ransom man pays for the capacity to be aware of his own suffering and that of his fellows and for the ability to envision ways to reduce that suffering by bringing about changes in the human situation. Erich Fromm referred to this creative aspect of suffering when he wrote: "If man has lost the capacity to suffer, he has also lost the capacity for change."[3]

I believe that some of the uneasiness that permeates our smiling society stems from our unwillingness to accept suffering as an essential part of life. This refusal, as Dorothee Sölle observes, "can result in a flight from reality in which contact with reality becomes ever more ephemeral, ever more fragmentary."[4] The willingness to accept suffering, on the other hand, brings us closer to reality and to the creative forces of renewal and change. Suffering that darkens our days may in this way generate more life and greater joy. It may even be held, as Dr. J. H. van den Berg suggests, that "happiness exists by the grace of a certain amount of unhappiness." Happiness, he surmises, "is the crowning glory of a life that has known pain and trouble. Though the most cherished moments give the impression of purity—and that is what they do—upon closer examination we find that that purity is the varnish, which is composed of elements stemming from less happy or even unhappy times in the past."[5] Happiness may also result from the shadows cast by future suffering, as is the case when we love more deeply because we realize that one day our beloved will die.

This life-generating, happiness-creating potential of suffering is not unlimited. Beyond certain limits, suffering is only dismal, destructive, deadly. The limits depend on the individual's ability to endure and absorb suffering, to learn from it and to be enriched by it.

Our age has produced massive suffering beyond the limits of endurance, suffering that was unbearable, suffering that did not create more life but only despair and death. One could hold that suffering in the death camps went even beyond the suffering of Christ on the cross, because in the camps the tormented had not only to suffer their own dismal fate but also to witness that of their husbands and wives, their parents and children.

There proved to be astonishing differences in people's ability to suffer. There were saints in the camps whose saintliness was pure suffering converted into more life. But the vast majority just perished. Any suggestion that their fate could have served a higher purpose, any theory imputing meaning to their fate, is blasphemous. Nothing could be learned from it except the depth of depravity of those who inflicted the suffering. It had no meaning except the meaning that a few of the sufferers were able to bring to it. It was this meaninglessness that made the suffering in the camps unbearable for all but a few of the victims. Only a handful shared the experience described by Viktor Frankl, himself a survivor of Auschwitz: "Suffering ceases to be suffering in some way at the moment it finds a meaning"[6] and he quotes Nietzsche's words: "He who has a *why* to live for can bear with almost any *how*."[7] Meaning, Frankl holds, can be found in the mere acceptance of suffering: "No one can relieve [the sufferer] of his suffering or suffer in his place. His unique opportunity lies in the way in which he bears his burden." Frankl speaks of "the courage to suffer" and remembers the men—I have a hunch that he was one of them—"who walked through the huts comforting others, giving away their last piece of bread."[8]

The demand to accept suffering is a demand one can make upon oneself only. Had Frankl made that demand on others he would have allied himself not with the sufferers but with their tormentors. To comfort—yes. To encourage—yes. But every sufferer must be left free to deal with his own suffering in his or her own way.

Another inmate who had that "courage to suffer" was the French author Jacques Lusseyran. Jacques was blinded in an accident at the age of seven. During the occupation of France he became a leader in the Resistance. He was nineteen years old when the Nazis caught him. In the concentration camp of

Buchenwald he tried to show his companions how to stay alive:

I could turn towards [my fellow-prisoners] the flow of light and joy which had grown so abundant in me. . . . Often my comrades would wake me up in the night and take me to comfort someone, sometimes a long way off in another block.

Almost everyone forgot I was a student. I became "the blind Frenchman." For many I was just "the man who didn't die."[9]

Jacques Lusseyran was an exception. So was Viktor Frankl. By accepting the reality of their suffering they overcame it and by overcoming it they found the strength to comfort others.

There were other exceptions. Some "entered [the] gas chambers upright, with the Lord's Prayer or the *Shema Yisrael* on [their] lips."[10]

Elie Wiesel mentions the little girl in the "silent . . . procession marching towards the . . . flames . . . undressing her little brother as she tells him gently, so very gently, not to be afraid, not to be afraid, for one must not be afraid of death."[11] What is there left to say? Words fail. This is the end.

It was the most extreme example of suffering inflicted by men and women on other men and women, and children. In the words of a Dutch survivor: "Everything that had become sacrosanct to humanity was trampled underfoot. No sick or helpless person, no child, no orphan was saved."[12] It was an extreme and gruesome example of other-inflicted suffering.

In less demonic forms, other-inflicted suffering is part of our daily lives. Because there are always those—and most of us will be among them at times—who feel that they gain by being cruel to others, who feel elevated by humiliating others, who try to overcome their own insecurity by destroying the security of others, who take revenge for imagined offenses, inflicting upon others the pain inflicted upon them.

There is also suffering that is self-inflicted. It is caused by a refusal to accept reality and by the assumption that happiness depends on changing the unchangeable. The father of daughters keeps telling himself and others that a son would have made him really happy; the father of sons finds that his life lacks perfection because he has no daughter. The woman who did not go to college makes herself miserable by comparing her actual position and salary with what these might have been if only she had had the advantage of a college education. "If only . . ." These are the words with which we create suffering out of our refusal to accept reality. If only I had been promoted. If only I had sold my securities before the recession. If only my wife had more social graces. If only my daughter had not met that unattractive boy. If only I could afford a Continental. If only taxes were reduced and salaries increased; if only we had no inflation.

This is self-inflicted suffering. How adroitly is this self-inflicted "if only" suffering used by the advertisers to make us buy their wares. How shrewdly do they arouse and exploit ever greater discontent to make us buy even more. Still, it is not beyond our power to outgrow this self-inflicted suffering, to leave it behind us as Paul left "childish things" behind him when he became a man.

Yet if we outgrow self-inflicted suffering and are spared other-inflicted suffering, we remain confronted with what might be called God-given suffering, the suffering inherent in the human condition. There will always be unfulfilled hopes, frustrated aspirations, shattered love, the loss of parents, children, and friends, sickness, and ultimate death. There will always be the ambiguity of our self-centeredness.

Arnold Toynbee describes self-centeredness as "both a necessity of life and at the same time a sin."[13] This ambiguity creates a lifelong quandary. We have the optical illusion that we are the center of the universe. We may try to reduce suffering by adhering to that illusion, by seeking to make the universe conform to our purposes, by ignoring our equality with others, and by avoiding confrontation with the real center of the universe that we call "God," that absolute Reality in which we live and move and have our being. In this effort to reduce suffering we move farther and farther away from reality, and ultimately perish in the prison of isolated self-centeredness.

Acceptance of the painful truth that we are not the center of the universe, on the other hand, and the recognition that the center is not in ourselves but in God, keeps us within the truth and enables us to experience both our relatedness to our fellow-men and our oneness with God. But the ambiguity persists. For, as Toynbee expresses it, the prison of our self-centeredness is not merely a prison from which we want to free ourselves but it is also our home, to which we must return from time to time lest we lose our identity.

We all have experienced this at some time. Someone has died, someone we loved very dearly. We do not want to be separated from that person; we want to stay with, to somehow merge our being into the being of, that person; but we discover that short of self-extinction it cannot be done. And a few hours after having felt desperate in our loss, we sit down for a meal to sustain our body; we return to the home of our self-centeredness.

Thus we walk the narrow ledge between the abyss of self-centeredness and the abyss of self-extinction. This ambivalence, this dualism, pervades the human situation. We cannot experience joy without pain, if only the pain of joy's finiteness. It is the pain felt by lovers, whose ecstasy in oneness cannot last because they must return to the prison homes of their selves. That is why the ultimate love story is the story of Romeo and Juliet. Their oneness in love was perpetuated in death. They left that narrow ledge of life. They did not return to their prison homes. As long as we live on that ledge we will suffer because, short of an act of sacrificial self-extinction, our love of God and man is bound to be imperfect.

Maybe that is why he who loved perfectly and made that sacrifice said of himself that "the Son of Man has nowhere to lay his head"; that is, he had no home; he had freed himself of his prison home of self-centeredness.

We are unable to follow him. We are unable to muster sufficient self-effacement, sufficient altruism, sufficient willingness to share everybody's burden. We do not feel up to it. We feel that we are already doing our share. We are afraid of loving more because we know that the more we love the more we suffer. For in a loving relationship we become participants in the suffering of the beloved. Passion implies compassion. The word is derived from the Latin prefix *cum* (co) and the verb *patior*, that is, to suffer. Compassion, therefore, is co-suffering. He who loves is a co-sufferer. That is why our ability to love is limited by our ability to suffer. That is why absolute love demands absolute suffering. This is one of Christianity's deep mysteries.

André Malraux points to this mystery when he says that early Christianity won the day in Rome because it told the sufferers that "Jesus . . . died in agony . . . so that you should not have to face this agony of yours alone."[14] That is, so that you should have a co-sufferer.

To know that one does not have to face it alone, that one has a co-sufferer, that is what was needed then, that is what is needed now. It is needed by those in the hospitals and the prisons, in the homes for the elderly and the mental institutions; and by those outside who are desperate and at the end of their tether, who do not know where to turn, who feel persecuted by poverty and illness, by the police and by the neighbors, by their obsessions and their fears.

I read a magazine article about a hospital that had been an amputation center during the war. It described the agonizing problems of physical and mental adjustment caused by the loss of hands, feet, arms, or legs. "For this reason," the article stated, "amputation centers maintained on duty status 'morale builders' whose work was of no less importance than that of the skillful surgeons; they were personally involved men, who gave advice from their own experience as amputees . . . and who were thus able to give the amputees a lift, mentally, morally and physically. Having suffered the same pains and anxieties, they could give comfort and solace to others."

A middle-aged couple who had lost their first child many years before befriended a young couple who had also lost their first baby. "We were able to comfort them," the older woman told me, "because we had experienced the same sorrow. There is an unseen fraternity of parents who have lost children."

She was right. There exists a mysterious community of sufferers. Albert Schweitzer has called it "the fellowship of those who bear the Mark of Pain."[15]

Miguel Unamuno extends this community to include all

mankind: "All living beings are united by suffering," it is "the universal or divine blood that flows through us all."[16]

Let us then accept suffering willingly, knowingly, as a means—the only means—to reach out to others, to comfort them, and to love them as ourselves.

9

✂

The Mystery of Redemption

And the angel said unto them, Fear not: for, behold, I bring
you good tidings of great joy, which shall be to all people.
For unto you is born this day in the city of David a Saviour,
which is Christ the Lord.

LUKE 2:10–11

God is there, too, in the desperation.
I do not know why God should strike
But God is what is stricken also:
Life is what despairs in death
And, desperate, is life still . . .

ARCHIBALD MACLEISH, *J.B.*[1]

The observance of Christmas began late—perhaps sometime
in the third century. It was a kind of liturgical afterthought
but its celebration became the great popular festival of
Europe throughout the Middle Ages. After the Reformation,
the observance of Christmas varied from country to country.
It was suppressed in Scotland, frowned upon in New England
until the nineteenth century, and looked upon with suspicion
by the Calvinist Dutch well into the twentieth century because the candles on the Christmas tree reminded them of
Catholicism.

Christmas and Easter share with the pagan festivities on
which they were grafted—the celebrations of the winter solstice and the vernal equinox—the elements of birth and death
and rebirth, of the new that is born out of the old, light that

comes forth out of darkness and overcomes that darkness. Christmas can be seen as the projection of the Easter event upon the story of Jesus's birth as we find it in the gospel according to Luke.² It is Luke's gospel that proclaims the tidings of great joy "for unto you is born . . . a Saviour which is Christ the Lord."

In these words lies a remarkable anachronism, for the designations "Saviour," "Christ," and "Lord" came to be applied to Jesus only after his death, symbolizing the interpretation given to the Easter event by the early church. Dag Hammarskjöld recognized the connection between Christmas and Easter when he wrote: "For him who looks towards the future, the Manger is situated on Golgotha, and the Cross has already been raised in Bethlehem."³

Most liberals do not recognize Jesus as "Lord" or "Saviour"; such messianic titles have no clear meaning for them. Lately, doubts have arisen in more traditional circles about the meaning of these terms and their applicability to Jesus. Thus the Catholic theologian Monica Hellwig submits that

Even to the Christian there is a most important sense in which Jesus is not yet Messiah. The eschatological tension has not been resolved. What may be expected in the messianic fulfillment has not yet become manifest in the world . . .⁴

Sister Charlotte Klein, another Catholic scholar, describes how this argument is developed by Gregory Baum and Rosemary Ruether. They hold that

It is historically not true that with Jesus of Nazareth the final messianic era has arrived or that the kingdom of God has been already established. . . . They ask that the person of Jesus be reinterpreted and that his own claims and the claims made for Jesus and his message by the churches be re-examined. . . .

The world itself has remained unredeemed: sickness, war, hunger, greed, and evil abound. The reign of God is not manifest. . . .

During the two thousand years since the coming of Jesus, the world and the hearts of humans have not radically changed. Jesus . . . has not transformed the world.[5]

Some seven hundred years ago a similar argument against Jesus's messiahship was raised by Moses Nahmanides, a Spanish-Jewish scholar. In a disputation that took place in the year 1263, he reasoned:

In Genesis Chapter 3, many are the penalties which Scripture records as falling upon Adam and Eve, such as: "cursed is the ground for your sake . . . thorns also and thistles shall it bring forth to you . . . in the sweat of your face shall you eat bread . . . for dust you are." And so also upon the woman does punishment fall: "in sorrow you shall bring forth children." Now, all these conditions endure even up to the present day and nothing of what is seen and experienced of them was cancelled by expiatory action in the time of your Messiah.[6]

Sister Klein suggests that "Judaism need not apologize for its unbelief in a Messiah who has already come without apparently renewing anything." She concludes that "we Christians shall have to work out a new answer to the urgent question: in what sense was Jesus the Messiah?"[7]

Ruether and Baum hold that, for the believer, Jesus is the paradigmatic human who has conquered evil by love. To many liberals that would be an acceptable definition. But it seems to me that it is not complete, that it leaves out a crucial aspect of his life. For it is of vital importance that, according to the criteria of this world, he was a failure. He suffered the agonies of those who, in the end, are utterly betrayed, defeated, and deserted. To him applied Isaiah's prophecy:

He was despised and rejected by men; a man of sorrows, and acquainted with grief. . . .
He was oppressed, and he was afflicted . . . like a lamb that is led to the slaughter. . . .
By oppression and judgment he was taken away. . . .
And they made his grave with the wicked . . . although he had done no violence and there was no deceit in his mouth.

"A man of sorrows, and acquainted with grief." Indeed, his was not a success story. Had he been a success, he would have been forgotten long ago. For it is out of the ambiguity of his worldly failure that Christianity was born. It is because of this same ambiguity that the question raised by Jesus himself, "Who say the people that I am?," is still with us today. Every age has tried to answer this question in its own way. Ruether and Baum, in our age, see in him a unique human being whom believers choose to follow. Do those who consciously have made that choice lead a more Christlike life? Who is to say, for, as Walter Muehl points out, the concepts of the Judeo-Christian religious tradition, which have formed and are the substance of Western civilization, "have worked their way so well into the conventional wisdom that few of the people who implement, benefit or suffer from their application are conscious of their origin."[8] This means, I believe, that one may be a Christian without knowing it and even in spite of denying it.

Still, those who knowingly follow his example place themselves in a special position with regard to the phenomenon of suffering. They accept suffering as an essential element in life's fulfillment.

One could say aphoristically that if the story of Job made suffering respectable, Jesus made it redemptive. After Job, suffering no longer had to be regarded as punishment for sins committed by the sufferer. After Jesus, suffering became potentially uplifting, liberating, enabling. For certainly only those who have suffered, those who are acquainted with grief, those who "have been there" can have an awareness of the suffering of others, can comfort them and help them bear their burdens.

In leafing through a book about baroque architecture, I came across the picture of an especially attractive small church built in that exuberant style. It showed the sanctuary, looking from the back toward the choir, with its richly ornamented organ framed by gilded carvings of ascending and descending angels. It was the church near Dachau, the site of one of Hitler's most infamous concentration camps. And I wondered: How was it possible that Sunday after Sunday, for years on end, people would go to mass and pray to God in this exquisite little chapel, while a few miles away the inmates of Dachau were being tortured and exterminated? Didn't they realize what was going on? No—they didn't.

But—did we? *Do we?* Are we sensitive to, are we aware of, the suffering that goes on around us? Maybe some of us are, sometimes. And to the degree that we are aware of it and act on that awareness, we are consciously or subconsciously following the example of him who taught his followers to be aware of other people's suffering, to overcome their innate self-centered and self-protective instincts, and to have compassion on those who are in need of it. He taught them the old commandment given to his people by Moses: "Thou shalt love thy neighbour as thyself." Indeed, "in him was life; and the life was the light of men."

The crisis of our days lies in the danger that the profusion of their evil will extinguish that light. The extent of that evil is only now slowly being realized even by those who were its witnesses if not its victims. Even the surviving victims have only recently begun to write books, publish diaries, and make their memoirs available. Only now, at the end of their lives, are they able to speak of the unspeakable they witnessed in their youth.

I received a letter from an old school friend of mine. We grew up together. In those days he was a devout son of the church. During the occupation of Holland he was taken hostage by the Nazis, and spent several months in the concentration camp of Amersfoort. After the war he became a leader in the movement for the unification of Europe. He wrote:

For our generation it does not make much difference whether one happens to have been in a camp or not. We have all of us been in the camps and we will have to live with that past. . . . "Amersfoort" represented to me, after a very sheltered youth, the first contact with what Dorothee Sölle calls "senseless suffering." It left me with feelings of hatred and sorrow. Strangely, the hatred disappeared. The sorrow stayed. Sorrow because human beings were able to do this to human beings. And then to be aware, somehow, that it was not only they, but that we, human beings, are able to do this to others. "Auschwitz" as a code word for all the unthinkable that happened there, represents the senseless suffering to which there is no metaphysical answer. The answer given to Job has become less and less acceptable to me. No Plan of Salvation, however redemptive, can wipe out or explain that suffering. "God after Auschwitz" is no simple matter, not for Job, nor for us.

Possibly the most scholarly of the books emerging now on the horrors of the Holocaust is Lucy Dawidowicz's *The War Against the Jews 1933–1945*. Shortly after its publication in 1975, a friend asked me what I thought of it. "If you have not read that book," I began to say, "you have not li . . ." I wanted to say "you have not lived" but I was unable to finish the sentence. "If you have not read that book," I said instead, "you have not died."

Most people do not want to die. Most people try to forget these horrors. Paul Fussell makes this point in an essay that opens with these lines by Siegfried Sassoon, written after the First World War:

> Who will remember, passing through this gate,
> The unheroic dead who fed the guns?
> Who shall absolve the foulness of their fate—
> Those doomed, conscripted, unvictorious ones?[9]

Fussell warns that "Germany would be delighted if we forgot Dachau, England if we forgot Suez, the United States if we forgot the Bay of Pigs, Chile, Cambodia."[10] He wants us to remember these things, to which we might add others, like John Kennedy and Robert Kennedy assassinated, Martin Luther King slain and "a boy dying on the Kent State University sidewalk, the black blood flowing out of his head."[11]

The world tries to forget these things. Some deny that they ever happened. One of those, Arthur R. Butz, declares that the Holocaust never took place. "I . . . became convinced," he writes, "that the legend of the several million gassed Jews must be a hoax. . . ."[12] The president of the German-American Committee of Greater New York wrote a letter to the *New York Times* in October 1977 protesting the intention of the New York public-school system to introduce a study program on the Holocaust. He said that by now it would be better to forget the whole thing; besides, he said, there is no real proof that the Holocaust actually did happen, and anyway it was not only the Germans who had committed atrocities; so had others.

The last observation is, of course, correct, though no act of genocide as revolting as that committed by the Nazis has ever disgraced civilization.

Sometimes these atrocities alluded in a demonic way—willed or unwilled, we don't know—to the life and death of Jesus. Lawrence L. Langer describes such a case, taken from Elie Wiesel's *Night:*

Three prisoners, two men and a young boy, have been "convicted" of sabotage within the camp and are sentenced to be hanged before thousands of inmates. One imagines the boy, a "sad-eyed angel" on the gallows in the middle, the older victims on either side of him, a grotesque and painful parody—though literally true—of the original redemptive sufferer; the sentence is executed and the prisoners are forced to march by the dangling bodies, face to face with their own potential fate.[13]

And then he quotes Wiesel:

The two adults were no longer alive. . . . But the third rope was still moving; being so light the child was still alive. . . .

For more than half an hour he stayed there, struggling between life and death, dying in slow agony under our eyes. And we had to look him full in the face. He was still alive when I passed in front of him . . . his eyes were not yet glazed. Behind me I heard a man asking:

"Where is God now?"

And I heard a voice within me answer him:

"Where is He? Here He is—He is hanging here on this gallows. . . ."[14]

Most liberals don't believe that Jesus was God. But it is just possible that, when he was hanging there, somebody asked the question "Where is God now?" and that someone answered, "There he is, hanging . . . there."

Many don't believe that Jesus was the Redeemer. But there is a mysterious bond between him and that child hanging on the gallows, and that boy bleeding to death on the pavement of Kent State University, and all those others who through the ages have suffered and in their suffering have wondered "Where is God now?" He may not have been the Redeemer, but two thousand years ago he taught us by his life and death that awareness of the fate of others, love to the point of self-sacrifice, is not beyond human reach.

He taught us that suffering is not something at the periphery of life, but something at its very core, something that is of its very essence. He may not have redeemed this world, but he lit a light of redemption.

10

⁂

The Courage to Be a Failure

The true prophets know . . . that ten successes that are
nothing but successes can lead to defeat, while on the contrary ten failures can add up to a victory, provided the
spirit stands firm.

MARTIN BUBER, *Israel and the World*[1]

The hope is in the faculty of wrongness, the tendency toward error. The capacity to leap across mountains of information to land lightly on the wrong side represents the
highest of human endowments.

LEWIS THOMAS, *The Medusa and the Snail*[2]

"The secret of success in life is known only to those who have
not succeeded!" When I stumbled on this aphorism of John
Churton Collins, I was not only charmed by its gentle and
wise skepticism but also struck by the fact that apparently
in his day, sometime around the turn of the century, "success
in life" had already become a generalized concept, no longer
connected with a specific endeavor. Throughout time there
have been successful—or, for that matter, unsuccessful—lawyers and musicians, housewives and plumbers. But the desire
to "be a success" in a general, nonspecific sense is, I believe,
something typical for our day and age.

Though typical, it is not easy to define what it means to
be a success. It certainly has a connotation of wealth—a successful individual in our society is not a poor individual.

It also has something to do with being popular, with being accepted by one's peers. The successful man or woman is happily married. The successful couple has a limited number of healthy, unproblematic, good-looking children. They are members of the local country club and are active in civic affairs. Furthermore, as Vance Packard, an expert on the subject, informs us, in order to make the grade your occupation must be that of a major executive of a large firm or a successful licensed professional with advanced degrees; your education must have flowered into professional or graduate-school attainment; your source of income must be preponderantly inherited wealth, and you must own two homes with fashionable addresses. You must be white, preferably of English extraction; you must have gone to the right schools, and in those schools have fraternized with the right people. You must have the right religion—Protestant, of course, but not just any form of Protestantism. The Episcopal church is right, Presbyterianism will do and so will the United Church of Christ. Unitarianism does not necessarily disqualify you, for though "tiny in total number, [it] outranks all denominations in the number of eminent Americans who have claimed it as their Church."[3]

If these are the requirements that have to be met, who of us can qualify as a "success"? Precious few, indeed. And what is the result? Massive frustration, which has become fertile soil for the activities of our eager advertising fraternity, these "merchants of discontent," as one of their own group has labeled them. They have become experts in exploiting this frustration by persuading us in a million different ways to surround ourselves with symbols of success: the right brand of car, the right kind of carpeting, the right style of blue jeans, which, in the words of a senior Wall Street analyst, "are a way for upwardly mobile people to gain status."[4]

[89]

The desire to appear successful has become a national obsession. To this end we work hard, go into debt, abstain from doing things we want to do and do things we don't want to do but are supposed to be doing. In the process we have given up our autonomy and have become dependent on what others think of us. We have become less interested in what we are than in what we appear to be. As Erich Fromm observes:

[We are] concerned with efficiency and success rather than with [our] happiness and the growth of [our] soul. . . . The "personality factor" takes precedence over skills . . . intangibles such as family background, clubs, connections and influence are also important desiderata. . . . To belong to a religion and to practice it is also widely regarded as one of the requirements for success.[5]

How do these standards for success affect man's attitude toward himself?

His feeling of self-esteem . . . depends on his salability on the market, or the opinion others have about his "attractiveness." He experiences himself as a commodity . . . if he is passed by while others are snapped up he is convicted of inferiority and worthlessness. . . . He is dependent on others for approval and in constant need of it; helplessness and insecurity are the inevitable results. Man loses his own identity . . . he becomes alienated from himself.[6]

This is the price we have to pay for "being a success."

I think the price is too high. It must no longer be paid. We must stop selling ourselves short. We must regain our independence and try to be successful not in a general, nonspecific way but in ways determined by ourselves, our talents, our

taste, our personality, and the unique conditions of ou
dividual life situation.

We may still strive to be successful but our idea of su.....
may not be that of the world. A salesman may be successful
not by selling more than his competitors but by telling the
truth about his merchandise; a stockbroker not by garnering
as many wealthy clients as possible but by once in a while
advising people who do not know where to turn because they
are not interesting as sources of commissions.

If you are told that a young girl at the age of twelve is able
to speak several words, it does not sound like a success story
until you are told that her name is Helen Keller. Then you
recognize it as the story of one of the most successful women
of the century. Success consists of overcoming our handicaps,
our weaknesses, our prejudices. We are successful when we
accept disappointment without being discouraged, when we
are patient instead of being irritated, loving instead of vin-
dictive. Success is achieved when people overcome their self-
centeredness and thereby become able to comfort those who
are in need of being comforted.

Paul admonished us, "Be not conformed to this world, but
be ye transformed by the renewing of your mind, that ye
may prove what is that good, and acceptable, and perfect,
will of God."

The renewing of our mind, the transformation of our being that enables us to prove what Paul calls "the good and
acceptable and perfect will of God," may make us successful
though the world may regard our success as failure.

This truth, that spiritual success may be worldly failure,
is deeply embedded in the Christian tradition.

When Nikita Khrushchev, late in his career, paid a visit to
the French capital, he was quoted in the press as having said:

There is much in Christianity which is common to us Communists. I only disagree on one point and that was when Christ said: "If I am struck on one cheek I will turn the other." I believe in another principle: if I am hit on the left cheek, I hit them back on the right cheek so strongly that the head may fall off. This is my only difference with Christ.[7]

It seems to me that the difference is essential. Khrushchev wanted to be a success on his own terms, but we are heirs of him who admonished his disciples, saying: "For what shall it profit a man, if he shall gain the whole world, and lose his own soul?"

We may strive to gain the world, to be successful in the world, without losing our souls. But if that proves to be impossible, we must be cheerfully prepared to give up that striving. We must have the courage to be a failure.

The early Christians had this courage. They were able to stand torture, to face destruction, and to go singing into the arena confident that their souls would be saved.

There exists failure that seems to be total failure. Failure that is not "offset" by the spiritual success of saving one's soul. Failure in a career, not because I did not want to cheat, not because I did not want to compromise, not because I resisted temptation. Failure just because I did not have what it takes. Or, possibly, because I had bad luck while the others had good luck. There is death not for a cause, not for a principle, not in order to defend something or somebody. Just death. Because a driver was drunk, or because a plane crashed, or because somebody worked harder and worried more than his heart could stand. There is failure in marriage. There is failure in rearing children. There is failure resulting from illness. That kind of failure is total. Nothing is saved by it: it is the kind of failure that makes the world look like a meaningless enterprise. It is the kind of failure that the man experienced who in his agony cried out: "My God, my God, why hast Thou forsaken me?"

We must bring ourselves to face even that failure.

And now we have entered the inner chamber of religion. It is empty here. Few people enter these days. The place is not popular even among our spiritual leaders. Here we are confronted with our failure, and the only way of being successful here is to find the courage to accept that failure, to surrender our self, to give up our ego, to relinquish our desire for worldly success. From this courage, from this willingness to let go what the world cherishes most stems the strength of the spirit.

This is the mystery that is embedded in all great religions, but in none so clearly, so unequivocally, as in Christianity.

The story of Jesus's life was the story of a gigantic failure, a failure of such dimensions that the Western world, spiritually speaking, is still living by its grace, the grace by which the poor in spirit are blessed, the mourners are comforted, and the meek shall inherit the earth.

When we have become successful in finding the courage to be a failure we shall have come home.

III

CONFRONTING

11

❧

A Bargain with God

And Abraham drew near, and said, Wilt thou also destroy
the righteous with the wicked?

Peradventure there be fifty righteous within the city;
wilt thou also destroy and not spare the place for the fifty
righteous that are within?

That be far from thee to do after this manner, to slay the
righteous with the wicked: and that the righteous should be
as the wicked, that be far from thee: Shall not the Judge of
all the earth do right?

And the Lord said, If I find in Sodom fifty righteous
within the city, then I will spare all the place for their sakes.

GENESIS 18:24–26

In the book of Genesis, we read how the Lord appeared to
Abraham and how Abraham bargained with him about the
destruction of Sodom and Gomorrah. This ancient story presents an essential aspect of man's relationship with God, of
man's position vis-à-vis the universe. For it raises the question
whether God has made man in his image or whether man has
made God in his. The answer to this question distinguishes
humanists from theists, and existentialists from those who live
within the Judeo-Christian tradition. This ancient tale, therefore, goes to the heart of unresolved theological and philosophical questions.

The Lord appeared to Abraham, we read, in the form of
three men. Are the three men together "the Lord," a kind of

anachronistic premonition of the Trinity? Or are they three heavenly messengers through whom the Lord speaks to Abraham, very much as the president of the United States might speak to a small Latin-American nation through a three-man delegation? Or is one of the three the Lord himself? This last theory finds some support in the continuation of the story. For after we have been told, in the last verse of the chapter, that "the Lord went his way," the first verse of the next chapter says, "And there came two angels to Sodom," the Lord himself having apparently returned to his heavenly abode. This version appeals to me also because it fits the old-testamentary belief that if you see the Lord (I suppose knowing that it is the Lord) you shall surely die. Abraham's inability to establish who of the three actually is the Lord thus would protect him from disaster.

Two modern analogies come to mind. A well-known German heart specialist sometime in the thirties received an invitation from the Russian government to come to Moscow to examine Stalin. The outcome of this examination could obviously have far-reaching political implications. Upon his arrival in Moscow he was taken to the Kremlin, where, during three successive days, he examined three mustached gentlemen who looked so much alike that any one of them could have been Stalin. One, I was told, had a heart condition.

In December 1964 Juan Perón made an abortive effort to return to Argentina from Spain, where he had been living in exile. The *New York Times* carried this item: "Juan D. Perón, the former Argentine dictator, boarded one of three planes in Madrid, all bound for South America."

One of three planes. One of three Stalins. One of three heavenly messengers. It is, however, in the bargaining scene that the story really comes to life. Abraham, after having won his point about the fifty righteous men, feels that maybe he has been overly optimistic in assuming that there are fifty righteous men in Sodom. Consequently he begins his carefully phrased, respectfully submitted but doggedly pursued bargaining to get the Lord down from fifty to forty-five ("wilt thou destroy all the city for lack of five?"; this is real genius in negotiating) , from forty-five to thirty, all the way down to ten.

Why did Abraham stop at ten? Three possible answers occurred to me. First: he may just not have dared to go further lest the Lord be irked. Second: the Lord had established a precedent when he destroyed mankind in the big flood, saving only Noah, his wife, their three sons and their wives—all in all, eight people. Abraham may have felt that if eight righteous men and women had not been enough to keep the Lord from destroying the wicked on an earlier occasion, he might run into trouble by going under ten. Third: among the Jews up to the present day ten is a minimum congregation; with fewer than ten you cannot have a service. Perhaps that is why Abraham stopped at ten.

Interesting as all this may be, it is inconsequential compared to the one statement Abraham makes before he starts bargaining, the statement that assures him success in dealing with the Lord by putting the Lord on the defensive: he, Abraham, the man, in the words of the Bible, "stood before the Lord . . . and drew near, and said, 'Wilt thou also destroy the righteous with the wicked? . . . That be far from thee to do . . . to slay the righteous with the wicked. . . . Shall not the Judge of all the earth do right?' "

Abraham is no longer asking his Lord; he is telling his Lord. He, man, is putting down the law, the law of right and wrong. This then brings us back to our original question, whether God has made man in his image or whether man has made God in his. The interpretation that Abraham was not asking the Lord but was telling him points to the latter version, to man making God in his image.

But another interpretation seems just as valid. Abraham, wanting to muster his courage to raise the question of right and wrong with the Lord, finds reassurance in reminding himself that, of course, the Lord, the "Judge of all the earth," is a righteous Lord and that, of course, it is far from him to slay the righteous with the wicked. The question remains unresolved.

Maybe this question, crucial as it seemed at the beginning, is less important than the fact that the story presents a rational dialogue between God and man. As such it is an eminently satisfactory story. There is an encounter between man and his maker and they agree on basics. They engage in a dialogue that is meaningful in its reasonableness, its logic, its terminology, which is essentially a human terminology applicable to earthly reality.

Is this what plagues us in our times? Not so much who made whom in whose image, but, rather, the question whether we are confronted with a divine reality in a meaningful way. Is there, in Buber's words, a "Thou" with whom the "I" has an encounter in terms that are those of a dialogue, a mutuality, and not those of a projection? The humanists do not think so. The theists do. The existentialists do not think so. The Judeo-Christian traditionalists do.

And then there are those who find themselves in a precariously balanced in-between position, which Herman Hesse described when he wrote some fifty years ago: "We become acquainted with that state of mind in which we are unable to decide whether the images on our retina are the result of impressions coming from without or from within." And then Hesse puts these words in his hero's mouth: "We create gods and struggle with them, and they bless us."[1]

But if God blesses us there is, again, a mutuality, an encounter, an I-Thou relationship. Then we have not created him but we have discovered him. Or possibly he has revealed himself to us. Who is to say?

Hammarskjöld wrote: "God does not die on the day when we cease to believe in a personal deity, but we die on the day when our lives cease to be illumined by the steady radiance, renewed daily, of a wonder, the source of which is beyond all reason."[2]

There is an ultimate reality, he seems to say, that does not depend on our specific beliefs, yet we depend on recognizing it, not necessarily in the form of a personal God but in standing before it in awe and wonder without comprehending its identity. If this is so we still exist by the grace of experiencing a confrontation.

Many of the troubles of our troubled age, many of the despairs of our despairing age, stem, I believe, from too many of us having lost this sense of confrontation. We often feel as Job felt when he exclaimed:

Oh that I knew where I might find him! . . .

Behold, I go forward but he is not there; and backward, but I cannot perceive him.

On the left hand . . . I cannot behold him; he hideth himself on the right hand, that I cannot see him.

However, Job's next words were: "But he knoweth the way that I take." This is exactly what many of us are no longer able to say, for we have lost that sense of confrontation to which Job clung with the tenacity of one who, in Hammarskjöld's words, believed that he would die if he lost it.

Abraham's encounter with God was an unproblematic one. Whether he told the Lord or asked the Lord, an agreement was reached that was highly satisfactory: the righteous would not be destroyed with the wicked.

Job's encounter with God was much more problematic because he, the righteous one, is made to suffer while the wicked prosper. And he prays to God: "Shew me wherefor thou contendest with me. Is it good unto thee that thou shouldst oppress, that thou shouldst despise the work of thine hands, and shine upon the counsel of the wicked?"

In this prayer we may discern the echo of Abraham's challenge to God: "Shall not the judge of all the earth do right?" In the end, of course, Job's faith in God's righteousness is vindicated. Job's story has a happy ending.

I believe that in Abraham's and Job's confrontations with the Lord we find certain elements of Jesus's confrontation with God.

Abraham shows concern for his fellow-men. He is not pleading for his own life but for the lives of the righteous men among the inhabitants of the two doomed cities. In the course of Abraham's bargaining with God an idea is developed, a principle is taking form, the principle that the wicked are to be saved for the sake of the righteous. For don't they agree, Abraham and the Lord, that even if there are only ten righteous men, the wicked will be saved for their sake?

In Job's encounter with the Lord another principle emerges, the principle that suffering is not punishment of the wicked but is a test of the righteous. Thus the concept of the "suffering servant of the Lord" emerges, the suffering servant whose advent, many centuries later, is prophesied by Isaiah and who, again many centuries later, makes his entrance upon the stage of history in the person of Christ. He suffers as Job had suffered, only, contrary to Job's suffering, his did not have a happy ending, at least not in terms of human history. As Abraham before him, Jesus pleaded with God to save the wicked, only it was not because he, the righteous one, wanted to live but because he, the righteous one, was willing to die. Contrary to what happened in Sodom and Gomorrah—and what had happened before in the Noah story—it was no longer the righteous who were saved and the wicked who were slain, but the righteous one who was slain that the wicked be saved.

This is the basic tenet of the Christian church. Its mystery has preoccupied man for two thousand years. Deeply anchored in it are the roots of all Western religion. The magnificence of Western civilization is its fruit. This mystery has been the source of man's profoundest confrontation, and the subject of man's most intimate dialogue, with God.

The trouble of our day is that man's dialogue with God as supervised and edited by the institutional church has gone stale. To many it has become, by and large, empty of meaning. John Robinson, Bishop of Woolwich, quotes these words from an interview of a girl of nineteen in the *London Daily Mirror:*

Q. Do you believe in God?
A. No. I used to, but not now. I don't see how there can be a benevolent God. There are too many tragedies—personal and in the world. . . . *Religion is disgusting.*[3]

In her answer, in her assumption that God has to be benevolent, we hear the echo of Abraham's and Job's dialogues with God. But this young twentieth-century girl no longer talks to God; she talks instead to the *Daily Mirror*. In the name of the newspaper there lies a striking, though unplanned, symbolism: the young girl talking to a mirror.

John Hayward speaks of those whose faith "is undercut by the facts of worldwide tyrannies and wars, by the seemingly ineradicable plight of refugees and displaced persons, by the reigns of terror and the means of violence ever poised to destroy the uneasy truce across the face of hostile continents."[4]

Albert Camus's Nobel Prize acceptance speech in 1958 most vividly recapitulates his generation's pilgrimage:

Those men born at the beginning of World War I, who had reached the age of twenty just as Hitler was seizing power and the first revolutionary trials were taking place, who then had to complete their education by facing up to war in Spain, World War II, the regime of the concentration camps, a Europe of torture and prisons, must today bring their children and their works to maturity in a world threatened with nuclear destruction. . . . Probably every generation sees itself as charged with remaking the world. Mine, however, knows that it will not remake the world. But its task is perhaps even greater, for it consists in keeping the world from destroying itself. . . . Starting from nothing but its own negations, [it] has had to reestablish, both within and without itself, a little of what constitutes the dignity of life and death.[5]

Camus is widely regarded as an existentialist atheist. I find his statement a deeply religious one. For in his suffering he felt confronted with a reality that made him take on the task to "reestablish . . . a little of what constitutes the dignity of life and death." The very experiences that destroyed his conventional religiosity compelled him to keep "the world from destroying itself," that is, to save the world. The suffering servant who dedicates himself to saving the world? It seems to me that this modern Job, in turning his back on God, found himself confronted with Christ. It is as if in Camus, the atheistic existentialist, Christianity has come full circle.

"Those who find no rest in God or in history are condemned to live for those who, like themselves, cannot live: in fact for the humiliated," he wrote.[6]

He who finds no rest in God—that was Camus himself, who, like Abraham, bargained with God but, unlike him, was unable to come to an agreement and, therefore, found himself "condemned," as he put it, to live for his humiliated fellowmen; that is, to live the Christlike life. His fate exemplifies the fate of many in his generation. For the point was not, in the end, whether he struck a bargain with God, but that he, an unbeliever, bargained with God for the sake of his fellowmen.

12

❧❧

Except Thou Bless Me

And Jacob was left alone; and there wrestled a man with
him until the breaking of the day.

And when he saw that he prevailed not against him he
touched the hollow of his thigh; and the hollow of Jacob's
thigh was out of joint, as he wrestled with him.

And he said, Let me go, for the day breaketh. And he
said, I will not let thee go, except thou bless me.

GENESIS 32:24–26

Existence is full of instances in which no meaning can be
found in suffering on the part of the suffering subject.

PAUL TILLICH, *Systematic Theology II*[1]

William E. Flowers was nineteen years old, bright and black.
They buried him on a beautiful fall day. In a way it was his
second burial, because he had died of suffocation when a
grave he had been forced to dig as part of a fraternity initia-
tion rite collapsed.

At the funeral mass the Reverend August Langenkamp expressed dismay that he could not preach a sermon that would
explain the meaning of Mr. Flowers's death. " 'I wanted to
give a good sermon,' he told the two hundred mourners
'. . . I don't know why I can't do it. I don't know why the
Lord didn't help me to do it.' "[2]

One possible answer to Langenkamp's question is that the
Lord leaves it to men and women to explain to other men

and women why he does certain things, why he permits certain things to happen. If this is so, it could be that some of those who are charged by him, or who by becoming members of the clergy charge themselves with the task of explaining all the strange things the Lord is doing, are running out of explanations. Maybe they are getting weary of explaining the unexplainable, of trying to find meaning in what so often appears to us to be meaningless.

Perhaps the whole thing is a bitter joke. What comes to mind are Robert Frost's good-humored lines:

> Forgive, O Lord, my little jokes on Thee
> And I'll forgive Thy great big one on me.[3]

But can one, with equal good humor, forgive the Lord his great big jokes on others? Who has that much good humor? Langenkamp, for one, apparently had run out of it. He was unable to forgive God. He was unwilling to pretend that he saw meaning in William Flowers's death. He was unable to justify the Lord's action.

This inability can also be explained in a different way: it can be interpreted as a lack of faith.

There is a passage in Albert Camus's book *The Plague* that supports this interpretation. In the plague-ridden city, a compassionate atheistic doctor and an equally compassionate Catholic priest have tried together to save the life of a little boy who has fallen victim to the plague. Their efforts fail. In the end, when, after several days and nights of agony, "the child was lying among the tumbled blankets, a small, shrunken form, with the tears still wet on his cheeks," the doctor says, "There are times when the only feeling I have is one of mad revolt."

"I understand," the priest replies, "that sort of thing is revolting because it passes our human understanding. But perhaps we should love what we cannot understand."[4]

The doctor, out of his atheism, accuses; the priest, out of his faith, justifies. Langenkamp, it seems to me, stands somewhere in between. I, for one, honor him for it. He may have felt dismayed that the Lord did not help him explain the meaning of William Flowers's death, but there may have been more comfort to the mourners in his dismay, his inability to justify, than there would have been in a justification.

John B. Wolf once described in a sermon the funeral of a child, one of several killed in a collision between a switch engine and a school bus: "While the Minister discoursed upon the text 'Death is swallowed up by victory,' the mother kept repeating bitterly, 'I only know my daughter is dead, I only know my daughter is dead. . . .'"

There is, I believe, a point of diminishing return in man's effort to explain, and thereby justify, the ways of God. The orthodox minister who preached on the text from Paul had, it seems to me, gone beyond that point.

It alarms me to find that many liberal ministers are doing the same, not by justifying those actions of God that seem senseless to us and sometimes even cruel, but by ignoring them, by pretending they don't exist.

In a Unitarian Universalist newsletter I receive, a "Sermon of the Month" quotes Emerson's words: "All I have seen teaches me to trust the Creator for all I have not seen." "Such a trust," the minister assures us, "brings us serenity of mind, unity of purpose, and the joy of living day by day in God's world. Yes, I believe in God."

Emerson was a spiritual and literary giant, but he may have been a giant in a small universe; most of us are small people in a giant universe. I, for one, though having lived a fairly sheltered life, know that what I have seen, and what I continue to see and hear and read day after day, does not necessarily teach me to trust the Creator for all I have not seen. Rather, it fills me with doubt and misgivings that sometimes border on despair.

It was in such a mood, though in a light vein, that I said to my wife one day, "If I am ever allowed in his presence, I will touch the hem of his garment, worship him, and then look up to him—or her—and say, 'Sir,' or 'Madam' (as the case may be), 'Would I be allowed to make a few suggestions?' "

In fairness to the trusting minister, I must mention his acknowledgment that "such a faith is difficult for some people to hold in these days of cold wars and hydrogen bombs; of graft and corruption, of cynicism and doubt." In fairness to my argument, I have to point out that the characteristics of our days, which he mentions, do not do justice to their agony. The Cold War may have been a dangerous political condition but it was certainly preferable to a hot war. The hydrogen bomb is a terrible weapon but it has, so far, not been used. Graft and corruption are regrettable but, to a degree, inevitable by-products of civilization. Cynicism and doubt are less regrettable, though equally inevitable by-products of the flowering of the intellect. I find it significant and alarming that his sermon does not mention a single one of the actual miseries of our world: no starving children, no dying soldiers, no fleeing refugees, no victims of torture— which I understand has become accepted practice in the majority of member states of the United Nations—no mistreatment of minorities, no genocide.

"This is not the first time in human history," states our

sermonizer, "when it is easier to be a pessimist than an optimist. And I see just as much evidence for my beliefs as the pessimist can produce for his." This may be so, but it is not the point. It is fine to have faith in the unknown blessings of the future; meanwhile it behooves us to take notice of the known evils of the present. That he does not do.

The newsletter quotes from another sermon: "We are living in an age of revolution. For centuries men have talked about equality and freedom. Now we are seeing them happen. A large part of our job is to guide this revolution by proclaiming the ideals toward which it is to move."

This statement about equality and freedom truly amazes me. I find it quite incredible. Doesn't he know that today eighty percent of the population of this globe lives under the rule of dictators of some kind and that the freedom of the remaining twenty percent, to which we—still—belong, is threatened by inflation, energy dependence, internal violence, electronic surveillance, and weak government?

Still another minister writes the following:

Here in the Church we meet one another for work, discussion and worship. Here we can get to know one another as persons. Here we do our own praying, singing, discussing. In meeting together we find greater strength. Contrast the person who isolates himself from people, has a few T.V. idols, to the person who dresses and goes out on the most miserable of mornings, walks, greets people, sings, prays and discusses!

True, I am quoting out of context. True, that is unfair since it may not do justice to the whole. My fear, however, is that these quotes are rather characteristic of the whole; a whole that tends to be patronizing, moralistic, self-serving, and smug; a whole that, at best, satisfies small needs but no longer relates to the depths and the heights of our lives; a whole that no longer speaks to man's ecstasy and to man's misery.

Man's misery. Man's God-inflicted misery. The kind of misery that made Langenkamp despair of the universe's meaningfulness. The kind of misery we like to think of as regrettable instances of disorderliness in an otherwise orderly system; something like a typographical error in an otherwise perfectly written text, or a once-in-a-lifetime accident like, for instance, death. But when we come to see in these accidents not the exceptions but the rules they represent, when we realize that these typographical errors are not errors but spell out a text of their own, then we begin to realize that we cannot ignore them, that we cannot be optimistic—or, for that matter, pessimistic—about their going away, but that in them we are confronted with something that goes to the essence of our existence, something that may very well be its very essence. Then one is tempted to argue, with Peter Berger: "The human condition, fraught as it is with suffering and with the finality of death, demands interpretations that not only satisfy theoretically but give inner sustenance in meeting the crisis of suffering and death. . . ."[5] In meeting, mind you, not in evading it. "There is a need," he writes, "for theodicy. Theodicy, literally 'justification of God,' originally referred to theories that sought to explain how an all-powerful and all-good God can permit suffering and evil in the world." It came to be used more broadly for "any theoretical explanation of the meaning of suffering or evil."[6]

The quest for this explanation is at the center of the religious enterprise. Without it we are playing Hamlet without Hamlet. This does not mean that our quest will be successful.

Indeed, we pursue it at the risk that its lack of success may ultimately lead us out of the realm of religion.

At a four-day symposium on the horrors of the Auschwitz concentration camp, held at New York's Cathedral Church of St. John the Divine in June of 1974, Emil Fackenheim stated: "Theodicy has gone up in smoke. The very attempt to justify the Holocaust and explain it is obscene."[7]

In these words one can hear the echo of a statement made by William James in the early years of this century:

It may indeed be that no religious reconciliation with the absolute totality of things is possible. Some evils, indeed, are ministerial to higher forms of good; but it may be that there are forms of evil so extreme as to enter into no good system whatsoever, and that, in respect of such evil, dumb submission or neglect to notice is the only practical resource.[8]

A remarkable text, especially if one considers that it was written before the two world wars brought Western civilization to the precarious position in which it finds itself today, before the world neglected to notice (to use William James's words) things like the murder of one million Christian Armenians by the Muslim Turks during the first of these two wars, the murder of six million Jews by the Christian Germans during the second one, the murder—perpetrated within a few days and hardly mentioned in the Western press—of four hundred thousand supposedly Communist Chinese by the Islamic Indonesians in the aftermath of that war, as well as the growing list of macabre events that followed. Remarkable, especially because of its supposition that "it may indeed be that no religious reconciliation with the absolute totality of things is possible."

For if this is true, if no such reconciliation is possible, we can, we must, forget about religion. Because religion—the word is derived from the Latin verb *religare,* that is, "to bind together"—consists of the very effort to reconciliate the totality of things.

Even if we come to the conclusion that the truth may be "comfortless and without ultimate meaning for human hope"[9] we are still in the realm of religion. But if we are no longer preoccupied with this quest for religious reconciliation with the absolute totality of things, if we abandon this quest, we may be philosophers, educators, teachers, social workers, and therapists but we are no longer ministers or, for that matter, religious laywomen and laymen.

The Bible is deeply preoccupied with this quest, from Job's challenge to God: "Shew me wherefore thou contendest with me," to Jesus' last words: "My God, my God, why hast thou forsaken me."

And then there is that very early story, the story of Jacob's wrestling throughout the night and giving out of his human nothingness this stubborn answer to his God, who wants to be released. "I will not let thee go except thou bless me."

May we have Jacob's stubbornness and wrestle with our God until he blesses us by justifying himself.

13

As a Tale That Is Told

We spend our years as a tale that is told. . . .
So teach us to number our days, that we may apply our
hearts unto wisdom.

PSALM 90:9,12

Religion is the awareness of the story dimension of life . . .
each person can become aware of the story each is telling
with his or her own life.

MICHAEL NOVAK, *Ascent of the Mountain, Flight of the Dove*[1]

To live is not easy. We spend a lifetime doing it and at the
end most of us are still not very good at it. It has always been
this way, but in our bewildering times possibly even more so
than at other times, considering the nuclear revolution, pollution, and computerization, the energy crisis, the food crisis,
the identity crisis, and the death of God, who, incidentally,
has turned out to be much less dead than originally assumed
by the so-called radical theologians of the fifties. When you
come to think of it, it is really quite remarkable how the individual lives through it all, suffers through it all, manages to
grope his way through it all, from cradle to grave, spending
the threescore years and ten or fourscore years allotted him
on earth, in the words of the psalmist, "as a tale that is told."

"As a tale that is told." In modern Biblical translations
these words are rendered in a different way. One translation
reads: "as a murmur"; another one: "as a sigh." I think it is

the modern translations' loss. What comes to mind is the story of the old New England lady who refused to buy a modern Bible translation, and expressed her loyalty to the King James version with the words "What was good enough for old Saint Paul is good enough for me."

As a tale that is told. Henry David Thoreau once wrote: "I am sensible of a certain doubleness by which I can stand as remote from myself as from another. . . . When the play, —it may be the tragedy of life—, is over, the spectator goes his way. It was a kind of fiction. . . ."[2]

As a tale that is told—a tale, a narrative, a story, a history, something that begins and from its beginning develops toward an end, something that has a past, a present, and a future.

Animals do not spend their years as a tale that is told. Loren Eiseley makes this point in his wonderfully wise and poetic way when he describes how he visualizes that man "crossed over" from the animal kingdom into the new invisible environment of the sociocultural world:

He was becoming something the world had never seen before—a dream animal—living at least partially within a secret universe of his own creation and sharing that secret universe in his head with other, similar heads. Symbolic communication had begun. Man had escaped out of the eternal present of the animal world into a knowledge of past and future. . . .

The Eden of the eternal present that the animal world had known for ages was shattered at last.[3]

The shattering of the "eternal present" of the animals, the knowledge of past and future, meant that "through the human mind, time . . . would enter . . . the world" and that the scene was set for history to develop, macro-history, the history of humankind or at least of large groups of women and men, and micro-history, the history of the individual, the story of a life, the tale that is told.

I think that all of us, at least intermittently, are aware of this historical quality of our lives, that all of us from time to time, as it were, step out of the present in order to survey the past, in order to refresh our memory of how we got where we are and to look down the road where we are going. Whether this historical reorientation fills us with sorrow or with joy, with gratitude or with resentment, with relief or with nostalgia, invariably it makes us realize that we are both creatures and creators, that we are neither masters of our fate nor its inane slaves, neither the sole authors of the tale of our lives nor merely its actors. This realization may create in us a sense of suspense and anxiety about the meaning of our lives. For not until the story is ended does it become evident what the story was all about; that end is uncertain. We can strive for a meaningful end, maybe I should say a meaning-giving end, but we may not be able to bring it about. For we are not in control of the unfolding of life, though we do control our reaction to its unfolding. It is that reaction that counts. It has enabled great leaders in times of crisis to mobilize the latent strength of nations by presenting contemporary events in the perspective of history.

This was how Winston Churchill's speech of June 18, 1940 before the House of Commons became the battle cry that called Great Britain to arms. His was a giant's reaction to a situation not of his making, a situation of such apocalyptic fatefulness that he could do justice to it only by stepping out of the present and dealing with the life of the British nation as a tale that is told: "Let us therefore brace ourselves to our duties, and so bear ourselves that, if the British Empire and its Commonwealth last for a thousand years, men will say, 'This was their finest hour.' "[4]

James Reston reminds us that in 1939, when "Neville Chamberlain was departing as Prime Minister and Winston Churchill was coming forward to take command, a loud cry went out across the House of Commons: 'Speak for England!' "[5] How well we understand this cry. For isn't that what we in our country have been yearning for? Leaders who can speak for America not only in terms of history but also in terms of the tale that is told. Because in the end, the tale, the story, the myth are the only means by which we can capture reality, define it, and come to terms with it. But it takes greatness to deal with the life of a nation as a tale that is told.

We find it hard to deal that way even with our own little lives. It presupposes a high degree of detachment and objectivity, an absence of self-pity, and a disregard of justified fear. For, in looking at our collective or individual lives in a historical perspective, we deal not only with an uncertain future but also with a factual past. That past may not be pleasant to behold. We may be fearful of recalling it.

I think this is one of the problems confronting black people in their effort to establish their identity. I was told that one of the projects of the Unitarian Universalist Black Caucus in the early 1970s was to send a number of young blacks from Syracuse to Zambia with the purpose of studying that country's native dance. This first struck me as strange until it dawned upon me that maybe they went there with the purpose of incorporating into their past the beauty of Zambia's dances. If this is correct, it would point to a desire to construct a synthetic past when the actual past is too painful to accept.

Hilary Ng'weno, a resident of Nairobi, seemed to justify this desire when he wrote:

Within a very short time, the Panthers and similar militant groups among blacks have succeeded in giving black people something even the late Dr. Martin Luther King, for all his abilities and devotion, never succeeded in giving them: a sense of pride in their own race and heritage. What does it matter that this sense of pride has sometimes been generated through emotional appeals to an oversimplified and glamorized image of Africa. . . ?[6]

I believe it does matter. Many of us, individually and collectively, find it troublesome to live with our real past, and therefore try to glamorize and beautify it retroactively by rewriting history. But it won't do. For in order not to live *in* the past, we have to live *with* the past, that is, our real, honest-to-goodness past. Any repression will haunt our subconscious, any distortion will haunt our conscience. Indeed, in order to be able to function in the present, toward the future, we must accept our past with all its shortcomings, with all its embarrassments, with all its frustrations, with all its shame. The remarkable success of Alex Haley's book *Roots* and the unique public response to the televised presentation of the story seem to point to the redemptive quality inherent in accepting rather than denying the past—however painful.

The commandment to honor father and mother may have been not only part of the tribal morality of a handful of nomads who roamed the Sinai desert some three thousand years ago; it may also have been a premonition of the psychological truth proclaimed by one of their descendants, Dr. Sigmund Freud, who taught that we have to accept our past in order to gain a future.

The fear of facing the past is not the only fear we have to overcome before we can step out of the present in order to see our lives as a tale. There is also the fear of being confronted with the future. At times all of us experience this fear, the fear of what the future may hold, its potential threats to our health and happiness and to the health and happiness of those we love. We do many things we really don't enjoy doing in order to make our future secure—as if this were possible—and we abstain from doing things we would enjoy doing because they might endanger our future.

I read the story of a Harvard student who was interviewed during the days of the student revolt in the late sixties. He said that he sympathized with the sit-ins, the occupation of buildings, and the destruction of furniture and files. When asked why he had not actively participated, he answered: "Well, me and all my friends all agreed with what SDS was doing. . . . But we didn't want to risk getting kicked out. Look, as long as you don't have anything permanent on your record you can change your mind later on in life about being a radical."[7]

Who can blame this Harvard man for wanting to keep all options open in an uncertain world? Meanwhile, he tampered in advance with his record of the future, as the re-writers of history tamper in retrospect with the record of the past.

The third and greatest fear we have to overcome before we can see our life as a tale that is told is the fear of being confronted with the intensity of life. There is a scene in Thornton Wilder's play *Our Town* that portrays such a confrontation. Emily, the young woman from Grovers' Corners who has died in childbirth, comes back from the grave to re-live her twelfth birthday. She has been warned that it will be more than she can bear but she wants to go through with it. We see her come down the stairs on the morning of her birthday. Her mother is waiting for her:

Well, now, dear, a very happy birthday to my girl and many happy returns. There are some surprises waiting for you on the kitchen table. . . .

But birthday or no birthday, I want you to eat your breakfast good and slow. I want you to grow up and be a good strong girl.

[Emily begins to open her parcels while her mother comments] That in the blue paper is from your Aunt Carrie. . . .

That in the yellow paper is something I found in the attic among your grandmother's things. You're old enough to wear it now, and I thought you'd like it. . . .

[Emily hears her father calling, off stage.]

Where's my girl? Where's my birthday girl?

Emily: *in a loud voice to the Stage Manager.*

I can't. I can't go on. Oh! Oh. It goes so fast. We don't have time to look at one another.

She breaks down sobbing. . . .

I didn't realize. So all that was going on and we never noticed. Take me back—up the hill—to my grave. But first: Wait! One more look. Good-by, Good-by, world. Good-by, Grover's Corners . . . Mama and Papa. Good-by to clocks ticking . . . and Mama's sunflowers. And food and coffee. And new-ironed dresses and hot baths . . . and sleeping and waking up. Oh, earth, you're too wonderful for anybody to realize you.

She looks toward the Stage Manager and asks abruptly, through her tears.

Do any human beings ever realize life while they live it?—every, every minute?

Stage Manager:

No.

Pause.

The saints and poets, maybe—they do some.[8]

None of us is a saint and few of us are poets. Most of us are ordinary human beings. We do not realize life while we live it. If we did we would not be able to stand it. But maybe, once in a while, when frustration and despair catch up with us, when we don't know what to do or where to turn, we may, in stepping out of the present and looking at our lives as the tale it is, find the strength to carry on toward a mean-ing-giving end.

14

❦

On Giving Thanks

O, tell us, poet, what you do?—I praise.
But those dark, deadly, devastating ways,
how do you bear them, suffer them?—I praise.
And then the Nameless, beyond guess or gaze,
how can you call it, conjure it?—I praise.
And whence your right, in every kind of maze,
in every mask, to remain true?—I praise.
And that the mildest and the wildest ways
know you like star and storm?—Because I praise.

RAINER MARIA RILKE, *Man and God*[1]

Most ministers have preached at least once during their preaching career what you might call the "Historical Thanksgiving Sermon," the Thanksgiving sermon that goes back to the first celebration of Thanksgiving, as described in William Bradford's *History of Plymouth Plantation*. In its puritan simplicity his description lends itself well to sermonizing. An orthodox minister may stress God's mercy in sending rain in response to fervent prayer, "shuch sweete and gentle showers," as Bradford notes, "which did so apparently revive & quicken ye decayed corne & other fruits, as was wonderfull to see . . ."

The liberal minister may be inclined to point to the hardships of that first winter, during which half of the group perished, which, in William Bradford's words, "was most sadd & lamentable." Sometimes two or three died in a day, so "that of 100 & odd persons, scarce 50 remained." After the rigors of that winter came the drought of the summer from the third week in May until the middle of July. While rain at the last moment saved some of the crops, the Pilgrims' position on the eve of the second winter was hardly enviable. The liberal minister may stress the human qualities of these men and women and the remarkable fact that this sorely tried group, this surviving remnant, felt moved to thank their God for the little they had. If they were so grateful for so little, how grateful should we not be for our plenty. That is the moral of both the more orthodox and the more liberal Thanksgiving sermon.

I have my quarrel with this moral; I find that it does not hold up under scrutiny. For when we say that it is wonderful that the Pilgrims were thankful for so little, we are really saying that we admire their modesty. But modesty is relative, and the question presents itself: At what price thankfulness?

Suppose a man who is interested in the stock market goes to a Thanksgiving service with a grateful heart. True, the Dow Jones Index stands at 800 as against 900 a year ago. He has lost some money but it might have been worse. So he is thankful with the Dow Jones at 800. But suppose the Dow Jones goes to 700? Will he still be thankful? Well, if he is very modest, maybe he will still be thankful. But what about 500? Who is *that* modest? Indeed, somewhere along the line we must assume that he stops being thankful, and around 400 he may well become quite angry with God for not looking better after his affairs.

Does this then mean that we must refrain from giving thanks for the good things in life? Certainly not. We can, with a good conscience, sing "the song of harvest-home":

[123]

> All is safely gathered in
> Ere the Winter storms begin:
> God, our Maker, doth provide
> For our wants to be supplied.[2]

But what we should realize is that it is not sufficient to be thankful when God does "provide for our wants to be supplied" but that we must be equally thankful when this is not the case, when we go through life with our wants unsupplied, when we carry with us unfulfilled wishes, unsatisfied desires, when there seems to be no happiness and peace but only hardship and struggle, anxiety and frustration.

It is pathetic to see how many try to be thankful not "because of" but "in spite of," not because their wants are supplied but in spite of the fact that they are not supplied. Still, when we come to think of it, we must admit that very often this "thankfulness in spite of" is ultimately a "thankfulness because of." For "thankfulness in spite of" is often based on the comparison of an admittedly unhappy situation in which we find ourselves with an even worse situation in which some real or imaginary other person finds himself. We are lying sick in a hospital bed, but we are grateful that we are not as sick as the person in the next bed. We are not happily married, but if we compare our married life to that of the people next door, we still have a lot to be thankful for. "It could be worse," we say.

This "thankfulness by comparison," as one might call it, is quite general. In van Eyck's painting "The Last Judgment," the heavenly bliss of the saved is accentuated by the portrayal of the infernal sufferings of the condemned. And it would not surprise me if among the condemned some were thankful because—however much they suffered—there were others who suffered more.

In the death camps, the man-made hell of the twentieth century, this principle was widely applied: people will suffer anything as long as there are others who suffer more, as long as they can tell themselves that they do not represent the lowest level of being, as long as they can feel superior to somebody else, as long as—in spite of their misery—they can be thankful that they are not one of those even more miserable ones.

This "thankfulness by comparison" is based on other people's suffering. The question arises, therefore, how ethical, how justifiable is it to be thankful for all we have, to count our blessings and relish their number when there are those who do not share in them and can count but few, if any, blessings of their own.

Surely we do not derive any added gratification from the plight of those on this globe who are living in poverty and slavery; nor are we as impervious to the fate of others as were van Eyck's heavenly elect, whose celestial felicity appeared more perfect by contrast with the suffering of those who had not made the grade.

Still, we do not hesitate to be grateful for all we have in spite of the fact that others do not have it. Maybe we should change the song of harvest home into a song of supplication, "God, our Maker, please provide for their wants to be supplied," thinking of the millions who are suppressed and starving and desperate throughout the earth. Indeed, do we have a right to be thankful as long as others are excluded from sharing in the blessings we enjoy?

The answer to this question, I believe, lies in the realization that thankfulness, while it may relate to specifics, has an absolute character. To give thanks is a basic human need, an essential element in our relationship to the universe. Thankfulness is independent of specifics. Still, because we are not abstract beings, most of us need something tangible to attach our thankfulness to. But these tangible specifics are, in a way, only the vehicles of our thankfulness; they are the media through which we fulfill this basic need of expressing thankfulness, not its objects. The thankfulness we express with regard to them stands for a greater, deeper, nonobjective thankfulness, thankfulness as a basic attitude of life. This basic thankfulness permeates our religious thinking, from Job's prayerful words "the Lord gave, and the Lord hath taken away; blessed be the name of the Lord" to Rilke's lines

> But those dark, deadly, devastating ways,
> how do you bear them, suffer them?—I praise.

There is a Jewish prayer that expresses this nonobjective, cosmic nature of man's need to be thankful:

> Blessed art thou, O Lord our God, King of the Universe,
> Who has kept us in life and hast preserved us,
> And enabled us to reach this season.

This prayer does not refer to specifics; it does not refer to the condition under which we exist; it refers to the condition of existence itself, to the condition of being. In this prayer, thankfulness is related to the most abstract and, at the same time, the most absolute man can conceive of; it is related to Life, to Being itself. "God, we thank thee that we are," that is what this prayer says, and we are reminded of the words Shakespeare put in the mouth of Henry VI:

> . . . O Lord, that lends me life,
> Lend me a heart replete with thankfulness![3]

Henry does not pray for things to be thankful for; he prays for thankfulness, and it is significant that he addresses his prayer to the life-giving God. "O Lord, that lends me life . . ." It is as if he equates being thankful with having life.

I believe that he is correct. And this brings us back to the Pilgrims. The sermonizers I mentioned earlier assume that the Pilgrims were thankful for having survived. It seems to me that they were able to survive because they were thankful.

15

Be Still, and Know

The present state of the world and the whole of life is diseased. If I were a doctor and were asked for my advice I should reply: Create Silence! Bring men to silence. The Word of God cannot be heard in the noisy world of today.

SÖREN KIERKEGAARD[1]

wild(at our first)beasts uttered human words
—our second coming made stones sing like birds—
but o the starhushed silence which our third's

e. e. cummings[2]

These lines from Whittier's hymn have always moved me:

Drop thy still dews of quietness,
    Till all our strivings cease;
Take from our souls the strains and stress,
And let our ordered lives confess
    The beauty of thy peace.[3]

Maybe it is because they express something we all long for: relief from life's burdens, elimination of the unessential, the superfluous, the things that distract and upset us, and achievement of a sense of order that makes life simple and noble and beautiful. We long for what the Greeks called *logos* (word, reason), the force that creates and maintains order in this world. The Hebrews called it *davar* (word, command). For it was God's word, according to the book of Genesis, that created order out of chaos: "The earth was without form, and void; and darkness was upon the face of the deep. . . . And God said, Let there be light: and there was light . . . and God divided the light from the darkness. . . . And God said, Let there be a firmament . . . and let it divide the waters from the waters."

In the book of Genesis God *spoke* the world into existence.

In John's gospel, merged elements of the Greek *logos* and the Hebrew *davar* are identified with Jesus as the Creator: "All things were made by him, and without him was not any thing made that was made. In him was life; and the life was the light of men. And the light shineth in the darkness and the darkness comprehended it not."

In this antithesis between light and darkness we may hear an echo of the Genesis story: "And God divided the light from the darkness. . . . " There seems to be a parallel between the story of creation in Genesis and the story of creation in the prologue to John's gospel.

Both start out with the words "In the beginning." Both recognize as vital to the creative process the element of separation: light from darkness, heaven from earth, land from sea, life from death, truth from untruth, meaningfulness from meaninglessness. Once this creative process has occurred— and only then—can we begin to speak of the order of things that stands in contrast to chaos, the formless void, "the deep," of Genesis out of which it was created.

Still, this order of things does not guarantee order in our lives. We are rooted in the order of things but our humanity gives us a certain independence from it. We may use this independence in ways that cause our lives to collapse into chaos; we may be able to regain a sense of order only if we are still and wait and listen to the *logos*-word.

Many in our day have lost this ability to listen, to wait, to be still. We suffer from what Henry IV, in Shakespeare's play, calls "the disease of not listening."[4] To us applies Jesus's saying "hearing, they hear not, neither do they understand." For the noise of our machines, our cars, our planes, the unsolicited music that pursues us in public places, the irrelevant chatter that pours out of our radio and television sets, have blunted our perceptiveness, dulled our senses, and trained us to hear without hearing and without understanding. Noise has become pervasive. Talk has become cheap, so cheap that we "leave it on" without listening to it. The degradation of music to background music was bad enough. Today we have—and some of us need—background talk while we go about our business. Cheap, senseless, meaningless, never-ending talk that is good for only one thing: it shuts out the silence. For we are afraid of silence.

The ancients recognized that it is in silence that truth is revealed. "Be still and know that I am God," says the psalmist. Be still and know. Stillness and knowledge. Stillness and insight. Stillness as the source of understanding. And he admonishes further, saying: "Stand in awe . . . commune with your own heart . . . and be still." The stillness has to be an awesome stillness.

The dictionary describes awe as "reverential fear, the feeling or emotion inspired by the contemplation of something sublime, a sense of profound admiration, respect, and reverence." The attitude of awe is the very opposite of the "so what" attitude that characterizes our age. Let us be frank: who of us has of late experienced reverential fear? Who among us has lately been moved by the contemplation of something sublime? And who remembers the last time when he sensed profound admiration, reverence, or respect?

The blind French author Jacques Lusseyran describes his response to Pablo Casals's playing of a Bach sonata in these words: "I listened to the sound. . . . It seemed to me the first sound I had ever heard in my life. But suddenly I caught myself listening to something else, something that moved me even more: the moments when he did not play. Those moments of silence interpreted clearly for me everything the music meant."[5]

Silence—awesome silence.

The French mystic Simone Weil, speaking of what she called "the Word of God," wrote: "The whole creation is nothing but its vibration. When human music in its greatest purity pierces our soul, this is what we hear through it. When we have learned to hear the silence, this is what we grasp more distinctly through it."[6]

Silence, audible silence.

And from here it is only one step to the devotional silence that has characterized the Quaker community from the days of George Fox:

> Still-born silence, thou that art
> Flood gate of the deeper heart.[7]

If we learn to overcome our fear of stillness, we may gain access to the knowledge of which the psalmist speaks.

Stillness may also deepen our understanding of each other. To commune in stillness will help us to communicate with words. Shared moments of stillness during conversations enable us to share the mood, the "preverbal" mood in which the meaning of words is rooted. For it is a common mood that gives words a commonly shared meaning. Without it, every conversation becomes a discussion, every discussion a debate and every debate a controversy.

The liberal religious dialogue suffers from the absence of a common vocabulary. There is insufficient agreement on the meaning of key words. As a result we find it increasingly difficult to speak about things of the spirit. Misunderstandings abound; the dialogue tends to become shallow. Its shallowness stunts the growth of the liberal religious community.

The causes that divide East and West contain similar elements. We do not share with the Communists mood or attitude or vocabulary. The same words carry different meanings in Moscow from those in Peking or Washington. It may not be by chance that the first fragile agreements on nuclear restraint, including the installation of the "hot-line" between Washington and Moscow, became possible at the Geneva disarmament conference of 1963, when a common mood prevailed, provoked by a common fear of an unintended ultimate catastrophe.

The microcosm of the family is affected by the same problem. Many parents and children no longer understand each other. Words are exchanged but there is no communication, no communion. Words have different meanings depending on whether they are used by parents or by their children. As a result, many children have given up listening to their parents in spite of their parents' urging "Will you please listen to me." Others, eager for clarification, interrupt their parents, in spite of their parents' admonition "Please let me finish."

But do we who are parents listen to our children? Do we make allowance for this difference in meaning of the words we exchange? Do we try to detect what their hidden meaning may be, how they may reflect the child's needs, the child's loneliness or despair? Do we respond to *their* plea "Please let me finish"? Or do we interrupt and dismiss them with mechanical and stereotyped remarks: "Take your elbows off the table," "Wash your hands," "Do not swear," "Have you finished your homework?," "Don't stay out late," and, worst of all, "Ask your father (or mother) ; I have no time now."

Few of us are good listeners. Otherwise we would understand that the words "Please let me finish" may mean a request for time. Time to experiment, to find out, to grow. It may mean a plea for confidence and trust: Don't judge me before I am ready to be judged. Give me time to make mistakes, to blunder. Have confidence that I will work out my problems. Trust me that in the end I will be able to stand judgment.

If we consider our lives in retrospect, most of us will find that on more than one occasion we have been in situations in which we needed time, time to straighten out something that had gone wrong, time to make amends, time to undo what we had done or to do what we had left undone. We were not ready to be judged; we were not ready to account for our deeds, and if asked to do so we would have pleaded, "Not now; give me time; have confidence in me. Please, let me finish." For the end may explain, justify, and redeem all that has preceded it. Judgment, therefore, should be suspended until the end has been reached, until the work has been finished.

Many of us have had the experience of looking over the shoulder of a painter at work. Few of us have been able to withstand the temptation to express premature judgment: "But the hill is not purple and the trees are not blue and what is that? I cannot even see what it is." Only to be told: "Give me time, let me finish." Even when that painting is finished, however, the painter will have taken simply one more step on

a long road of becoming, of evolving, of growing. That painting must be seen and appreciated and understood in the context of the artist's entire work, which, in turn, must be and
can only be evaluated in relation to the work of contemporaries and to all that went before and to all that will come
afterward. All of us are part of that creative process of which
Paul said, "It groaneth and travaileth in pain together." It
groaneth and travaileth—it is bringing forth, it is being born.
It is being born within us, it is being born around us. But
we are not aware of it, we do not understand it, we cannot
fathom it. Instead of heeding the psalmist's words "Stand in
awe . . . commune with your own heart . . . and be still,"
instead of listening, we, out of our finiteness, take it upon
ourselves to judge the infinite. It makes no sense, we say. It
has no meaning; life is meaningless; it is a bad joke, and God
is but the echo of our own voice that comes back to us out
of a universe that is dark and cold and empty.

From this point on and out of this mood, one road leads to
the existentialists, the aristocrats of the world of despair who
write meaningful books about meaninglessness, and another
road to their hedonistic counterparts who find solace in alco-
hol and drugs, and still another one to the false prophets of
race and creed and color, the prophets of futility—the cult-
ists, the Klan, and the neo-Nazis. All these groups and all
these movements and all these people have one thing in common: they speak and write; they make propaganda and try to
persuade; they fill the air with the noise of empty words, of
arguments and counterarguments, promises and threats, premature judgments and ill-founded prognoses. In the words of
Jesus, "They think that they shall be heard for their much
speaking."

Religious liberals contribute their fair share to this noise.

We are, as much as any other group, in need of that reverent silence, of that preverbal mood in which the meaning of words is rooted, lest our words, too, become empty. The same silence that may lend meaning to our words may permit us to listen to our hearts.

"Wash thy soul with silence," said Rabindranath Tagore.[8] Wait and be still. Shut out the noise and the haste, the frantic activity, the motion that leaves no room for emotion. In the stillness you will come face to face with the eternal mystery and from that confrontation derive faith and hope and vision. Only when we are still and wait, empty of desire, will truth come to us and will we be ready to receive it.

"In silence and in stillness," teaches Thomas à Kempis, "a devout soul profiteth, and learneth the hidden things. . . ."[9] Let us be still and know . . . and let us give God a chance to finish.

IV

TRANSFORMING

16

The Brighter Light

And the light shineth in darkness;
and the darkness comprehended it not.

JOHN 1:5

What I must do is all that concerns me,
not what the people think.

RALPH WALDO EMERSON, Self Reliance

In the spring of 1956 representatives of twenty-nine nations convened in Bandung, Indonesia, nations some of which were small and some immense, some with new names unknown only a few years before and others with names as old as civilization. They had one thing in common: they were awake after having been asleep; they were independent after having been foreign-dominated; they were participants in the dynamics of world politics that had been the monopoly of Western nations for centuries. It was the first conference of what we have since come to call the "less-developed countries." Their number has increased to ninety-two. Their ever-increasing population represents the poor three-quarters of the world.[1]

This upsurge of "the masses," as Ortega y Gasset prophetically called them in the late twenties, is not confined to the emergence of these new nations. The population of the industrialized countries has shown not only a similar increase in number but also a continuing growth in the percentage of the population that actively participate in the process of civilization. As a result of the emancipation of women, these active participants doubled, so to speak, overnight. The farmers were a nonparticipating group until the Model T Ford brought them out of their isolation. The Depression of the thirties, the Second World War, and the subsequent era of prosperity and decentralization of wealth, coupled with a tremendous development in transportation, communication, and mass entertainment, have by now made of almost every inhabitant of the industrialized countries an active participant.

What does this mean? It means crowded cities, crowded roads, crowded subways and planes, beaches and parks, and an ever-diminishing opportunity for the individual to be alone. It means we have been weaned from aloneness. Aloneness is not fashionable. It is frowned upon. If you want to be alone you are antisocial, a bad sport; you are not a regular guy. For regular guys live and move and have their being in groups: Rotary or Kiwanis clubs, country clubs or similar associations. The expression "to go it alone," which used to carry a connotation of proud independence, has taken on one of social failure. Loners are suspect. One is supposed to be group-minded, to conform, and to avoid being conspicuous.

A student at the University of Nebraska College of Law, the first freshman ever to chalk up perfect grades in all his classes, was asked whether he would like a perfect year as a sophomore. According to the *New York Times,* he answered, "I should say not. It makes you too unpopular."

A study about pre-teenage reading habits records the following from an interview with a twelve-year-old girl:

The little girl: I like Superman better than the others because they can't do everything Superman can do. Batman can't fly and that is very important.
Question: Would you like to be able to fly?
The little girl: I would like to be able to fly if everybody else did, but otherwise it would be kind of conspicuous.[2]

There you have it, the fear of going somewhere others do not go.

Gertrude Crampton's children's story *Tootle* illustrates how we foster that fear.[3] Tootle, the young engine who is taught "always stay on the track, no matter what," discovers the delight of going off the tracks and finding flowers in the field. Tootle wants to do "his thing." The citizens of the town, however, get together to teach Tootle the lesson that little locomotives should stay on their track and follow the green lights. When he promises that from then on he will, he is cheered by the citizens and his teachers, who assure him that he will grow up to be a big streamliner.

We teach our children that it is not in their interest to go off the beaten path, to leave the track and pick flowers in uncharted meadows. We teach them to "follow the green light" and "all will be well." But there remains a grave question which the Tootle story blithely ignores: Where do these green lights lead and who put them there in the first place? And there does not seem to be any concern about the possibility that even if the green lights are properly placed, somebody may come along one day and switch those lights around. It seems to be taken for granted that the green lights will always lead in the same direction and to the same goal as "the true Light, which lighteth every man that cometh into the world," the Light that is glorified in the gospel of John. But that is not always so and when the wicked men come and change these lights around, only those who are guided by that True Light will escape their doom.

In the spring of 1935 I spent a few days in Berlin on a business trip. The Nazis had won one of their great prewar triumphs, the return of the Saar territory to the Fatherland. The occasion was to be celebrated with a huge torchlight parade. The management of the hotel where I was staying had advised foreigners to keep off the streets that evening. They were offered a chance to view the spectacle from the hall overlooking the avenue, Unter den Linden. Since my room happened to be on that side of the building, I decided to watch from there.

What I saw that evening was terrifying. It started even before I had seen anything, for while the wide avenue was still empty under the darkening evening sky, I heard a faraway murmur, as if a tide were coming in. The murmur came nearer and grew louder, blending two distinct noises: the steady march of tens of thousands of army boots and the singing of those who wore them. Singing is not the right word; it was a hoarse chanting in short, abrupt, rhythmic sounds that reverberated between the rows of buildings. And there they came swinging around the corner, torches in hand, ten, fifteen, twenty men in a row, a black flood. When they were passing under my window, still chanting, I could distinguish the obscene words about Jewish blood dripping off their swords and about the coming German domination of the world.

I don't remember how long I stood there, fascinated and nauseated. I do remember that in the end I sat down on the edge of the bed in that hotel room, feeling utterly alone, alone and frightened: Was it possible that these millions had all gone mad and that I was sane; was it possible that this whole huge city, one of Western Europe's great capitals, had come under the spell of some crazy obsession, and that I was free of it? But that couldn't be; of course the millions were right, they had to be right; millions could not be wrong.

I remember that I waited, seeking enlightenment, and I remember how after some time I suddenly knew, knew without a vestige of doubt, that I in my solitude was right and that they, the millions, were wrong. I was certain of it. In spite of my fear I felt the exhilaration of the discovery of truth.

During the years that have passed, I have often thought about this experience in the light of what was to follow. One aspect continued to puzzle me: It is obvious that those millions whose chants I heard that night could not all be bad. They were probably good fathers and husbands, loyal friends to each other, well adjusted within their own system, good mixers, wonderfully trained to follow the green lights that their leaders had installed for them—Tootles all, staying dutifully on their tracks—and the only trouble was that those tracks and those lights led in the wrong direction; the only trouble was that nobody seemed to remember that True Light of which John spoke, the one Light that supersedes all other lights. And if some remembered it, they did not have the strength to follow it, for that True Light may lead us away from the green lights and off the tracks, away from the masses and into solitude. For he who was that great light had the courage to be alone: conformists do not die on crosses.

Most of us are afraid of being alone. Still, it is in solitude that man feels closest to his Maker. Alone he has received his deepest inspiration. It is in solitude that the Saints heard the Voices, sensed the Spirit and saw the Light that enabled them, in turn, to speak to those who did not hear and see for themselves.

Moses was alone, keeping his flock on Mount Horeb, when he received the call to deliver the children of Israel. It was in solitude that he spent forty days and forty nights on Mount Sinai when he was given the law.

We read that forty days spent in solitude in the desert preceded the years of Jesus's ministry. And throughout those short years he sought periods of solitude to commune with the Spirit, to receive strength and inspiration from the Source of All Being.

On one occasion even Jesus did not have the courage to be alone. We read that, at Gethsemane, he took with him Peter and the two sons of Zebedee and said to them: "Tarry ye here, and watch with me." While he prayed, the disciples fell asleep. But he could not face his ordeal alone and woke them up: "What, could ye not watch with me one hour?" And when once again they fell asleep, "for their eyes were heavy," as Matthew expresses it, he found the courage to make the final decision in solitude, and from that moment on he remained alone.

The word "alone" is derived from the middle English *al one,* that is: entirely, wholly one. Aloneness, therefore, stands for al-oneness and points to the mystical experience of man's oneness with God, of wholeness and holiness. But the wholeness that is gained in solitude leads back to the multitudes. The Saints may derive holiness from being alone but they can only express it in their relationship with other human beings. Similarly, the insights man gains in solitude can only find expression in his relationship with others, in a growing awareness of their needs, in sharing their joys and sorrows, in trying to comfort those who are desperate, to make life more tolerable for those who suffer, and to strengthen those who follow the green lights away from the True Light. They must be encouraged to say "no," to go against convention, to defy the masses and, if need be, the law. They must be helped to walk alone, to think for themselves, to pray in solitude, to resist responding with conditioned reflexes to lights set up by they know not whom. They must be helped to find the courage to be alone and in their aloneness to grow into the consciousness of their oneness with him who was that True Light as bearers of his spirit and heirs to the Kingdom.

17

A Heavenly or an Earthly Kingdom

"Tsar Lazar, of honourable stock,
Of what kind will you have your kingdom?
Do you want a heavenly kingdom?
Do you want an earthly kingdom?
If you want an earthly kingdom,
Gird on your swords . . .
And drive out every Turkish soldier.
But if you want a heavenly kingdom
Build you a church on Kossovo. . . .

The Tsar chose a heavenly kingdom . . .
He built a church on Kossovo. . . .
Then the Turks overwhelmed Lazar . . .
And his army was destroyed . . .
And the goodness of God was fulfilled.

OLD SERBIAN POEM[1]

"Of what kind will you have your kingdom? / Do you want a
heavenly kingdom? / Do you want an earthly kingdom?"
The question put before Prince Lazar at Kossovo is still with
us today. Even in the year 1389 it was not a new question. For
the same choice had been given some thirteen hundred and
fifty years earlier by Jesus to the Rich Young Man. Contrary
to Prince Lazar, he opted for the earthly kingdom. When he
was told, "Sell all thou hast and distribute among the poor
and thou shalt have treasure in Heaven," he was unable to

[146]

give up his earthly treasures, for, as we read, "he was very rich."

A hundred years after Kossovo, the monk Savonarola preached the message of the Heavenly Kingdom in the streets of Florence and shocked the princes of the House of Medici and the citizens of that exuberantly worldly center of the Renaissance by reminding them of Jesus's teaching: "For what shall it profit a man if he shall gain the whole world and lose his own soul." Another hundred years later Marlowe raised the question in his drama *Dr. Faustus*. In our day Thomas Mann wrote his book of the same name, and, in between, more than twenty authors and various composers wrote books, dramas, and operas on the subject of Faust, who sold his soul to the devil in order to inherit the earth.

Do you want a heavenly kingdom or do you want an earthly kingdom?

The question is still with us. It is with us when we fill in our tax return and wonder whether or not to include that little commission we received in cash. It is with us when we make up our expense account and try to rationalize the inclusion of that nonbusiness dinner at which we entertained our private friends. It is with us when we tell our wives that tomorrow we will have to work late, or our husbands that this afternoon we have to go to a meeting of the hospital library committee, when on both occasions we are going to be otherwise preoccupied. It is with us when we ask the real-estate broker in strict confidence and solely for the sake of our neighbors—for personally we are free of prejudice—not to sell that house on our block to a black family. It is with us day by day in a multitude of situations when we bargain away a little piece of the heavenly kingdom for a little piece of the earthly kingdom, when we sell a little bit of our soul for a little bit of the world. Thus soul and world are in constant conflict.

There are moments of great peace, fleeting moments when soul and world are in harmony. These moments show what life *could* be, as against the way life *is*. They give a glimpse of the heavenly kingdom that is the hope of the earthly kingdom. But after these moments of harmony, the dynamics between soul and world resume their either/or quality, the quality that demands choice.

One such choice, which has confronted men in times of war, is that of conscientious objection. I know men who were conscientious objectors in the Second World War and in the Korean War and in the Vietnam War. I have admired these men. They stuck to their guns, the guns of the heavenly kingdom, in refusing to man the guns of the earthly kingdom. I have admired them for their courage, their consistency, the independence of their minds, the strength of their convictions. They represented an essential aspect of the public conscience. Without them there would have been no witness to the greatest of all commandments: Thou shalt not kill. However, it seems fair to say that they could, with impunity, adhere to their moral position of being unwilling to kill only because the majority of their contemporaries took the immoral position of being willing to kill—and to be killed. If, in a future war, the minority of conscientious objectors ever grows to the point of becoming a majority, then it seems to me we will have reached the stage in which conscientious objection can no longer be indulged in with impunity, the stage in which we will be faced with the same question that confronted Lazar on the plain of Kossovo: "Of what kind will you have your kingdom? / Do you want a heavenly kingdom? / Do you want an earthly kingdom?"

And if at that time we follow his example and choose the heavenly kingdom, then, in the words of the Kossovo poem, "the goodness of God [will be] fulfilled." But the Nazis, the Russians, the Chinese, or whoever wants to annihilate us at that time, will take over as the Turks did at Kossovo and subject us to the treatment supposedly suggested by General von Schlieffen, the German Chief of Staff around the turn of the century: "Take everything away from the vanquished, leaving them only their eyes to weep with."

How moral is it at all times to be moral? Rebecca West ponders this question in her book *Black Lamb and Grey Falcon.* " 'Lazar was wrong,' I said to myself, 'he saved his soul and there followed five hundred years when no man on these plains, nor anywhere else in Europe for hundreds of miles in any direction, was allowed to keep his soul. He should have chosen damnation for their sake.' "[2]

It is easy to criticize the government for spending uncounted billions for defense and to say that it would be better if that money were used to abolish the slums. Of course it would be better, but the troublesome question arises whether this is possible without endangering our survival. It is easy to say that you are against modern technology and mass organization, but what do you do by the time there are almost two hundred twenty million people in this country, going on three hundred million? Most of us are against a new Consolidated Edison plant being built in our community, not to speak of a nuclear power plant. But who of us is willing to abolish air-conditioning or reintroduce the candle to read by at night? A chancellor of the State University of New York observed in a commencement address that "an increasing number of young persons look at much of . . . scientific and technical change with suspicion, distaste and sometimes with utter revulsion—even while they promptly adopt its penicillin and computers, its jet planes and birth control pills."

John Gardner makes this point when he describes a visit to a scholarly friend:

He sat in an air-conditioned study. Behind him was a high-fidelity phonograph and record library that brought him the choicest music of three centuries. On the desk before him was the micro-film of an ancient Egyptian papyrus that he had obtained by a routine request through his university library. He described a ten day trip he had just taken to London, Paris and Cairo to confer on recent archaeological discoveries. In short, modern technology and social organization were serving him in spec-tacular ways. And what was he working on at the moment? An essay for a literary journal on the undiluted evil of modern tech-nology and large-scale organization.[3]

Do you want a heavenly kingdom? Do you want an earthly kingdom? Make up your mind, for you can't have both.

Some time ago I had a talk with a young scholar. In our conversation he commented on our foreign policy and criti-cized what he called our opportunistic attitudes. Our foreign policy, he said, should be based on moral considerations rather than on purely self-serving ones. When I asked him whether he felt that we could afford to be guided solely by moral considerations, he did not understand what I was talk-ing about. He said, "Maybe we should take the risk that goes with a moral foreign policy." Kossovo all over again. He was ready to opt for the heavenly kingdom at the risk of losing the earthly kingdom, the majestic structure of Western civil-ization, with its music and its literature, its paintings and its science, its cathedrals and its technology, but above all with greater liberty for more people than any civilization past or present has offered mankind, a civilization that far from being exhausted is presently suffering great pains of self-renewal, a civilization that is laboring to find new forms in which it can express and bring to fruition its great inherent potential.

It is true that many of our institutions have become obsolete, many of our structures neglected, many of our practices ineffective. But it is also true that there is a growing realization that this is so. There is a growing number of men and women, especially among the younger generation, who dedicate their lives to serving our society by reforming it, and in doing so serve the world at large.

Dr. Jonas E. Salk is reported to have stated that "mankind is in the midst of a transition from an epoch of competition and individualism to an epoch of cooperation and interdependence."[4]

Michael Novak describes his vision of the world to come in these words:

There must be, one day, an alliance between cultures describing themselves as "capitalist" and as "communist," for there is increasingly only one world and there must one day be one culture. Such a culture must be rich in diversity, not homogeneous. It must be open to alternatives and possibilities, not closed. It must be a culture of many philosophies, many theologies, many varieties of economic and political theory and practice. . . . Truthfulness, respect, difference, a capacity to listen—these are the modes by which human dignity expresses itself. Short of them, there is no dignity.[5]

Our world is laboring to renew itself without betraying its basic values. But it will take time. Meanwhile, I agree with Rebecca West that we must risk our souls in the process of defending and rebuilding and transforming our earthly kingdom, of which we are not the owners but the trustees for the benefit of our children and grandchildren, rather than risk that earthly kingdom in order to save our souls as Prince Lazar did on the plain of Kossovo.

I spoke of Faust, the symbol of Western man, who sold his soul to the devil in order to gain the world. In the original version Faust ends up in hell. It was Goethe who gave the Faust story a new and happy ending. For in the end, and in spite of his arrangement with the devil, Faust is saved because of the good he has done in this world. May it be given to us to hold our world together toward a better future, and may we, too, be judged worthy of salvation.

18

※

The Vertical and the Horizontal

For [Christoph Blumhardt] . . . the Kingdom of God is
a call for the transformation of the whole life. To the social
activist who has no inner life, no personal commitment to
the God of the inner temple, and to the Pietist who has no
commitment to the promotion of righteousness in the institutions of the public sphere, he would say: A plague on
both your houses; each of you has spatialized the work of
God, and thus has reduced the God of all life to a demonic
and dangerous idol.

JAMES LUTHER ADAMS, *On Being Human Religiously*[1]

What does it profit, my brethren, if a man says he has faith
but has not works? Can his faith save him? If a brother or
sister is ill-clad and in lack of daily food, and one of you
says to them, Go in peace, be warmed and filled, without giving them the things needed for the body, what does it
profit? So faith by itself, if it has no works, is dead.

JAMES 2:14–17

James's admonition that "faith by itself, if it has no works,
is dead" is clearly a call for action, social action. As such it
was frequently invoked in the fifties and sixties by those who
held that the church had become introverted, subservient to
the secular establishment, and insensitive to the misery and
injustice abroad in the world. With James they demanded
deeds, not words.

I submit, however, that at some other time, James might
have found it necessary to remind his flock that works without

[153]

faith do not save either, that indeed works by themselves if they have no faith are also dead. For the fact of the matter is that faith and works depend upon each other, that the one without the other is, in the end, bound to be subverted for the benefit of the ego. Faith without works tends to exclude others and to become pietistic and self-serving. Works without faith tend to make objects out of others and to become exploitative and self-aggrandizing.

The relationship between faith and works can be expressed in spatial terms, in terms of the vertical and the horizontal. In this metaphorical design, the vertical stands for our relationship with the mystery of the universe, our relationship with God. It is the dimension of the spirit. The horizontal signifies our relationship with our fellow-men; it stands for our involvement in the world. It is the secular dimension.

The vertical and the horizontal, the dimension of the spirit and the dimension of the world, faith and works. The cross they form was widely used as a symbol long before the advent of Christianity. In ancient Egypt, for instance, a hieroglyphic in the form of a cross whose upper part was pear-shaped stood for the word *ankh,* which in the language of Pharaonic times meant "life." The cross was the sign of life.[2]

Even within the Judeo-Christian tradition the cross can be made to yield a symbolic meaning other than that of the suffering and death of the Christ. This meaning can be derived from the answer Jesus gave when he was asked: "Teacher, which is the great commandment in the law?" He said: "You shall love the Lord your God with all your heart, and with all your soul, and with all your mind. This is the great and first commandment. And a second is like it, You shall love your neighbour as yourself. On these two commandments depend all the law and the prophets."

This answer in Matthew's gospel consists of the combination of two passages from the Old Testament, one from the book of Leviticus, one from Deuteronomy. Seen in this perspective, the cross could be given a symbolic meaning derived from the Torah, signifying the two axes that define the space in which we live: one vertical, love of God, the dimension of faith; and one horizontal, love of man, the dimension of works.

Love of God. To many these words may sound archaic and without substance. In the mind of others, they may even arouse hostility, as James Luther Adams suggests, because, "for some . . . the word 'God' is not the sign of reality but of a powerful illusion."[3]

To me "love of God" means devotion to the source of all life, by which we can transcend our ego-selves and through which we are—in love—related to all life and all being outside ourselves. Thus interpreted, love of neighbor is derived from love of God. The reverse is also true: in loving our neighbor we love God. But this is only so if we accept the definition of the word "neighbor" Jesus gave in the parable of the Samaritan: our neighbor is not somebody we like, somebody we admire or are beholden to, not somebody who might one day be useful to us or who happens to be living next door. Our neighbor is anybody who needs us.

This love of neighbor is not something that comes naturally. It is something that expresses itself in deeds done for no other reason than for the love of God. Often these deeds will infringe upon our immediate interests and preference. It may mean that we have to get up in the middle of the night when we want to sleep, to attend a meeting when we want to go sailing, or to baby-sit next door when we want to go to the movies.

I am reminded of a quotation from an unknown source that deals with Sainthood and its causes:

Why were the Saints Saints?

Because they were cheerful when it was difficult to be cheerful; patient when it was difficult to be patient; and because they pushed on when they wanted to stand still, and kept silent when they wanted to talk and were agreeable when they wanted to be disagreeable.

It was quite simple and always will be.

In doing these things the Saints became Saints.

In trying to do these things men and women become human.

Our civilization has shown marked variations in the degree to which individuals and society as a whole have identified either with the vertical dimension of the spirit or with the horizontal dimension of the world. There have been times of strong worldly integration and spiritual disintegration, and, conversely, times when, oblivious to the world, the individual has lived deeply integrated in the things of the spirit.

The Middle Ages may have witnessed the highest vertical integration of Western society. The individual's life from cradle to grave was, down to the smallest detail, related to Jesus's birth, life, death, and resurrection as taught by the church. The Gothic cathedral's surging arches symbolized that integration. Thousands of statues of men, women, and children, saints and sinners, angels and demons, flowers and animals, were blended into the contours of these amazing architectural expressions of religious devotion. The cathedral seemed to carry the world toward heaven in a devout gesture of consecration, signifying the church's grandiose effort to transform the spirit of the world into a World of the Spirit.

The effort failed. The spirit of the world prevailed. Under the surface of its splendor and magnificence, the late medieval church became secularized. It still flowered in great beauty, but it was no longer the spiritual beauty of the Gothic age; it had become the worldly beauty of the Renaissance. The vertical lines of the Gothic cathedral were succeeded by the arches and domes of the rediscovered classical Roman architecture, which, in turn, were succeeded by the convoluted lines of Baroque's worldly extravagance. Men and women awakened from the heavenly dream of the Kingdom of God and found pleasure in the earthly reality of the kingdom of man.

The church followed the trend of the day and the mood of its communicants. No wonder that it became estranged from the spirit of its founder. For he had spoken of a kingdom that was not of this world. He taught that the world must be overcome, that worldly things are incidental to spiritual things: "Seek ye first the Kingdom of God, and his righteousness; and all these things shall be added unto you." At the same time he went out into the world and used the strength derived from the spirit for the support of his fellow-men. He went out to heal, to comfort, to counsel, to teach. He loved his neighbor. He dealt with the world without becoming subservient to it, because his life in the secular dimension was derived from and supported by the dimension of the spirit.

We, however, are children of the Renaissance, which witnessed the beginning of the contraction of the vertical realm of the spirit. This process continued until, in our days, the vertical structure has collapsed. Yeats wrote in the 1920s:

> Things fall apart; the center cannot hold,
> Mere anarchy is loosed upon the world.[4]

[157]

In commenting upon these lines, Robert Kegan writes:

Of the things that fell apart, the most important was our connection to a super-sensible reality. The vertical thrust to life came crashing down, and the thud, deprived of the third dimension, spread itself over the skin of the earth. "We are down where all ladders start," Yeats again, "in the foul rag-and-bone shop of the heart." Confronted with a horizontal world, this flatland, this North Dakota uninformed by superhuman direction, twentieth-century folk ask the existential question: "Given that there is nothing 'up there,' what is down here?"[5]

This is the urgent religious question of our day. Various schools of existential thought result from efforts to answer it. But I want to question the premise: Are we really uninformed by superhuman direction? Is it true that the collapse of the vertical thrust of life leaves us deprived of the fruits of what was once experienced as "supersensible reality"? I do not think so. There are those who would agree with me. Let me give a historical example.

On January 25, 1950, Alger Hiss was convicted of perjury. On that day Dean Acheson, then Secretary of State, held a press conference during which he was asked whether he had any comment on the Alger Hiss case. He said:

. . . whatever the outcome of any appeal which Mr. Hiss or his lawyers may take in this case I do not intend to turn my back on Alger Hiss. I think every person who has known Alger Hiss or has served with him at any time has upon his conscience the very serious task of deciding what his attitude and what his conduct should be. That must be done by each person in the light of his own standards and his own principles. For me there is very little doubt about those standards or those principles. I think they were stated for us a very long time ago. They were stated on the

Mount of Olives and if you are interested in seeing them you will find them in the 25th Chapter of the Gospel according to St. Matthew beginning with verse 34.[6]

Dean Acheson, it seems to me, did not feel "uninformed by superhuman direction." He did not share the desperate resignation expressed in Yeats's lines:

> Now that my ladder's gone,
> I must lie down where all the ladders start
> In the foul rag-and-bone shop of the heart.[7]

Many of us, however, do. And we ask ourselves: Where do we go from here? Is there any place to go? Can a tolerable relationship between people exist without support from the spirit? Can there be love of neighbor other than that derived from love of God? Many philosophies have been contrived, many religious speculations dabbled in, many ways of life tried out in an effort to solve this existential question. They express the deep despair of our age as well as its shallow optimism. Despair stemming from the misconception that the vertical structure that collapsed was identical with the truth it stood for. But it was not; the truth survived. Optimism stemming from the misconception that any structure built in that vertical dimension of the spirit represents truth. But it does not; God is elusive.

Yeats meanwhile admits:

> Players and painted stage took all my love,
> And not those things that they were emblems of.[8]

The things they were emblems of, the things they stood for, the things they symbolized. Those are the very things our spiritual heritage is made of. Those are the very things that continue to give us "superhuman direction." We should hold on to them; we should continue to commit ourselves to them, forgetting the "players and painted stage," for to most of us those players and that stage have long ago become unbelievable.

This leads to the paradox of modern liberal religion: most of us have no concept of God. Is he/she/it "up there," as the Bible maintains? "Out there" or "beyond there," as Bishop Robinson proposes? "Down there," as Paul Tillich seems to suggest when he equates God with the "ground of being"? Most of us have given up making guesses about the nature of God. But this does not mean that we have given up our commitment to symbolic concepts like the "Fatherhood of God" as expressing the equality of all men and the dignity of the individual, and the "brotherhood of man" which derives from it.

The twenty-fifth chapter of Matthew, by which Dean Acheson felt directed, reads in part:

When the Son of Man comes in his glory, and all the angels with him, then he will sit on his glorious throne. Before him will be gathered all the nations, and he will separate them one from another as a shepherd separates the sheep from the goats, and he will place the sheep at his right hand, but the goats at the left. Then the King will say to those at his right hand, Come, O blessed of my Father, inherit the kingdom prepared for you from the foundation of the world; for I was hungry and you gave me food, I was thirsty and you gave me drink, I was a stranger and you welcomed me, I was naked and you clothed me, I was sick and you visited me, I was in prison and you came to me. Then the righteous will answer him, Lord, when did we see thee hungry and feed thee, or thirsty and give thee drink? And when did we see thee a stranger and welcome thee, or naked and clothe thee?

And when did we see thee sick or in prison and visit thee? And
the King will answer them, Truly, I say to you, as you did it to
one of the least of these my brethren, you did it to me.

I would be surprised if there were many readers who could
give credence to the story of the things that will happen
"When the Son of Man comes in his glory, and all the angels
with him. . . ." To most of us the idea of a last judgment
in which we are rewarded for services rendered on earth, or
punished for the omission thereof, is unacceptable. The
framework in which Jesus's teachings are given has lost credibility. But the teaching is there. We must learn to distinguish
between the framework and the message. The framework may
be obsolete; the message is timeless. The framework may be
relative; the message is absolute. Absolute and ultimate. We
may—and some feel that we must—rid ourselves of the framework but we must hold on to the message. It is our "superhuman direction." It represents the only hope for the future
—yes, the only hope for *a* future. For in it is rooted man's
concern for his fellow-man, his awareness of his neighbor's
need, his feeling of responsibility for his brothers and sisters
in the ghettos and the hospitals, in the prisons and the mental
institutions, for his brothers and sisters who suffer and are
in pain throughout the earth.

It is as if we had to take precious stones out of obsolete and
worn settings. Do away with the settings—but cherish the
stones. "For I was hungry and you gave me food, I was thirsty
and you gave me drink, I was a stranger and you welcomed
me, I was naked and you clothed me, I was sick and you
visited me, I was in prison and you came to me." Don't say,
"But that is only normal human behavior." For it is not.
Greece, for all its splendor, and Rome, for all its grandeur,

did not know about this kind of behavior, and our days have shown how gruesome "normal human behavior" can be.

The civil-rights confrontation in Selma could never have happened if somebody had not one day proclaimed that it is good "to set at liberty those who are oppressed." And organizations such as Alcoholics Anonymous, it seems to me, result from the direction given in the story of the Samaritan. No Samaritan, no Alcoholics Anonymous. I don't say that if Jesus had not spoken these words, some other human being, enlightened by the spirit, might not have spoken them, but I do say that these redemptive events could not have happened if the words had not been spoken. And I do say that other redemptive events will not occur unless these words are remembered. For faith can express itself only through works and works will not endure unless they are expressions of faith.

This brings us back to our topic: our vertical structure has crumbled. I hold that this occurrence has not compromised the vertical dimension of the spirit or invalidated its truths. I hold that it is our task to rededicate and commit ourselves to these truths, to recognize them as having been begotten by the spirit and to have faith that the crumbling of the structure of the spirit will not deprive us of the blessings of its grace.

19

Spring, Exodus, Resurrection

The wind bloweth where it listeth, and thou hearest the
sound thereof, but canst not tell whence it cometh, and
whither it goeth: so is every one that is born of the Spirit.
                                                      JOHN 3:8

The new is created not out of the old, not out of the best of
the old, but out of the *death* of the old. It is not the old
which creates the new. That which creates the new is that
which is beyond old and beyond new, the Eternal.
            PAUL TILLICH, *The Shaking of the Foundations*[1]

To many liberal ministers and congregations Easter Sunday
is a yearly recurring embarrassment that they find hard to deal
with. For the resurrection is not their "bag." Still, we share
with our more orthodox brethren and sisters the phenomenon
of the full church on Easter Sunday. Social custom apparently
outweighs the fear of embarrassment.

Various forms of worship have been developed in an effort
to avoid the issue. The most widely accepted one is the observation of Easter as a spring festival, as the celebration of the
reawakening of nature. Historically this can be justified. For
the Christian celebration of the resurrection was, as it were,
superimposed upon the pagan spring festival.

Sir James Frazer says of this and other similar superimposi-
tions: "The coincidences of the Christian with the heathen
festivals . . . mark the compromise which the Church in the

hour of its triumph was compelled to make with its vanquished yet still dangerous rivals." He speaks of "the supple policy, the easy tolerance, the comprehensive charity of shrewd ecclesiastics, who clearly perceived that if Christianity was to conquer the world it could do so only by relaxing the too rigid principles of its Founder, by widening a little the narrow gate which leads to salvation."[2]

It is interesting to observe how, after nearly two thousand years, many of us still try to use that extra little space by which the narrow gate was widened to slip through this Christian structure without Christian credentials.

Frazer's "shrewd ecclesiastics," meanwhile, were not the first to superimpose new celebrations upon older ones. For Passover, according to the *Columbia Encyclopedia,* in pre-Mosaic time may have been a spring festival only, and Peter Berger seems to agree when he writes: "The Passover originally . . . the feast celebrating divine fertility, becomes the celebration of the exodus."[3]

There exists, therefore, an analogy between the Jewish commemoration of the exodus, the deliverance from the yoke of Egypt and the Christian commemoration of the resurrection, the deliverance from the sting of death. Both were originally spring festivals.

There is also an intertwining, for the early Christians were Jews. To them the celebration of the resurrection was superimposed not on a spring festival but on their Jewish exodus-Passover celebration. In our Judeo-Christian tradition, therefore, there are three layers of celebrations: the first one is spring; the second one, exodus-Passover, and the third, the resurrection.

Spring, exodus, resurrection. All three have one quality in common; another is shared by Passover and Easter, and a third one is peculiar to Easter only. All three celebrations have in common the quality of renewal. The fertility cults of the ancients abound with resurrected gods or demigods symbolizing this renewal as an awakening from death. This is surprising. One would have assumed that, living close to nature, the ancients would have had a strong sense for the difference between the dead tree that remains leafless in the spring and the dormant but very much alive tree that develops new foliage. For spring is not a resurrection of life from death but a renewal of life within life. How new a renewal? Not very new, for spring is a yearly recurring event, a biological event that is predictable and holds no surprises. Thus, there is renewal but it is renewal without change.

The Jewish Passover and the Christian Easter are festivals of renewal as change. They celebrate events that have a unique as against a repetitive character, a spiritual as against a biological character. They celebrate changes in the human situation brought about by men who assumed seemingly superhuman tasks, after having wrestled with and overcome agonizing doubts about their ability to fulfill these tasks.

There is a dramatic analogy as well as a dramatic difference in the ways Moses and Jesus decided to take upon themselves their tasks of renewal. In the book of Exodus we read that when the Lord appeared to Moses in the burning bush and commanded him to go to Pharaoh and obtain the release of his people, Moses, who in his own words was "not eloquent . . . but . . . slow of speech, and of a slow tongue," replied in a stuttering voice: "Who am I that I should go?" and he resisted his Lord's demand for the better part of fifty-nine verses. In the end Moses gave in but not before the Lord had allowed him to take his brother Aaron along, his big brother Aaron, of whom the Bible says that he could "speak well."

The three synoptic gospels concur in their description of Jesus's decision. The scene is the Garden of Gethsemane. No God speaks out of a burning bush. In the end it is Jesus himself who answers in the affirmative his prayerful question whether he has to go. His loneliness is complete. Even his disciples, whom he has asked to stay awake while he is praying, fall asleep. And when the final chapter of the drama begins, they flee, leaving him without any human support in his final agony.

Passover celebrates man's courage to strive for freedom and live by saving his life. Easter celebrates man's courage to give up his freedom and live by losing his life.

Passover celebrates what is in this world and of this world. Easter celebrates what is in this world and not of this world.

Passover celebrates delivery from captivity and the hope to enter the promised land. Easter celebrates surrender into captivity and the hope to enter the Kingdom of God.

Spring, exodus, resurrection.

Easter as renewal. Easter as renewal and change in worldly reality. Easter as renewal and change in worldly and spiritual reality.

I believe we should celebrate all three.

Spring. I emphasized its foreseeable, nonchangeable character. Thornton Wilder, in his play *The Skin of Our Teeth,* gives a somewhat different reading. He depicts the coming of the ice age as if it happened just like that—one day spring just did not appear; it remained cold and it kept snowing and the glacier moved into the back yard and man realized that spring cannot be taken for granted, that spring is a yearly recurring blessing of which we are apt to forget that after all nobody owes it to us.

Many years ago Rachel Carson warned that one day spring

might come in deadly silence. Today, with our greater awareness of what we are doing to our environment, with our fears
—often exaggerated but essentially justified—that we may be
upsetting an existing balance of things by irreverent careless-
ness, we have more reason than earlier generations had to
give up our thoughtless "so what" attitude toward the blessing of spring and to celebrate its advent, as did those whose
dependence on nature was more evident than is ours.

Exodus. I mentioned the trouble the Lord had to persuade
Moses to go. No less significant was the trouble Moses had to
persuade his people to go. It took time to convert their resignation to slavery into a desire for freedom. Doubts about the
merit of this conversion lingered in their minds. When they
were encamped on the shore of the Red Sea—so the Biblical
story goes—and threatened by the chariots (our present-day
tanks) of Pharaoh, who had changed his mind and wanted
his slaves back, the Israelites in their terror

clamoured to the Lord for help and said to Moses: "Were there
no graves in Egypt, that you should have brought us here to die
in the wilderness? See what you have done to us by bringing us
out of Egypt! Is not this just what we meant when we said in
Egypt, 'Leave us alone; let us be slaves to the Egyptians'? We
would rather be slaves to the Egyptians than die here in the
wilderness."

Leave us alone. Is there anybody who has not heard these
words again and again? Is there anybody who has not spoken
these words again and again?

Most of us used these very words when Martin Luther King
challenged us to go and join the ranks of those who fought to
abolish the racial scandal in our midst. Most of us use these
words today when we are told to go and do something about

our abominable prison system, the disgrace of our mental institutions, the outrage of the slums, the perpetuation of poverty in our midst. Leave us alone, we say, because we are busy, slaving day and night to make money to pay our bills, to keep our marriage together, to get into the country club, to have fun. Change? What do I need change for? Leave me alone and if you want change, let somebody else do it. Who am I that I should go?

When I was about ten years old, I was taken to church for the first time. In the fashion of the times the minister preached on a biblical text that he analyzed and took apart and commented upon and put together again. His text on that day was taken from Jesus's parable of the sower, "A sower went out to sow his seed." And after having analyzed it and taken it apart and commented upon it and put it together again, he asked: "What are the most important words of our text?" and answering his own rhetorical question he said: "The most important words are: 'The sower went out,' because if he had stayed home, nothing would have happened." The sower was willing to go.

Passover is the celebration of going out and making things happen and bringing about changes. Passover celebrates man's courage to leave known dependence for unknown independence, the safety of servitude for the hazards of freedom. It is always safer to stay home. The Passover reminds us that we have to go out, that we must dare to face a strange world, that we must have the courage to be strangers. And out of the realization that we are strangers in a mysterious universe not of our making is born the urge to find an answer to the question why we are here.

In Psalm 119 we read:

Open thou mine eyes, that I may behold
wondrous things out of thy law.
I am a stranger in the earth: hide not
thy commandments from me.

If Adam had stayed home, nothing would have happened. He was "thrown" out of Paradise, in the sense in which farmers use that word when they speak of a colt that is "thrown" by the mare; possibly in the sense in which Martin Heidegger uses that word when he says that man is "thrown into being."[4] It was the birth, not the fall, of man. The flaming sword marks the beginning of our pilgrimage as strangers in this earth.

Noah embarked on his voyage leaving behind the familiar and the known. Abraham left the land of Ur and became a stranger in the land of Canaan. In the book of Deuteronomy, Moses commands his descendants to "make response before the Lord your God, a wandering Aramaean was my father," as if to wander as a stranger on the face of the earth was the mark of holiness. Joseph was a stranger in Egypt. Jesus was born on the road, in the stable of an inn. His life was that of a traveling teacher. During the short time of his ministry he went from one place to another, a stranger everywhere.

Ultimately, Passover celebrates man's ability to have faith and the courage to act out of that faith.

Jesus acted out of faith when he found the courage to sacrifice himself in order to bring about a change in this world. This change is symbolized in the Easter story of the resurrection.

Was the resurrection a real, physical occurrence? Most of us don't believe that. I, for one, don't. Many of us would agree with Peter Berger that "the resurrection . . . is no longer regarded as an event in the external world of physical nature, but is 'translated' to refer to existential or psychological phenomena in the consciousness of the believer."[5]

As I read the Bible, Paul did not believe it either. In his first letter to the Corinthians he addresses himself to "some among you [who say] that there is no resurrection from the dead." And then—and this is very significant—while affirming what was to become the basic tenet of the church, "if Christ be not raised . . . your faith is . . . vain," he emphasizes the difference between that which dies and that which comes to life, comparing it to the seed that perishes in order to bring forth the grain (observe the spring motif), exclaiming in the end:

So also is the resurrection of the dead. It is sown in corruption; it is raised in incorruption;

It is sown in dishonour; it is raised in glory; it is sown in weakness, it is raised in power;

It is sown a natural body, it is raised a spiritual body. . . .

And then with a tremendous emphasis, as if he wants to make the nature of the resurrection clear for all times, he repeats: "There is a natural body, and there is a spiritual body," thus pointing to the essence of the resurrection. It is not the renovation of something old but the transformation into something new: through a process named "death" corruption becomes incorruption, dishonor becomes glory, weakness becomes power. And a searching question arises: Is it possible that the real significance of the resurrection might be, not that weakness can become power, but that the only real power is the power born of weakness? And the only incorruption, the incorruption born of corruption? And the only glory that born of dishonor? Is this possibly the essence of the Christian message? Could it be possible that the meek will inherit the earth not because of their meekness but because the highest sovereignty is that born out of meekness? And the highest good that born of evil?

There are phenomena in our society that seem to point in that direction. Think of Alcoholics Anonymous. Only former alcoholics can help their alcoholic brothers and sisters. Reform of our antiquated prison system depends on the cooperation of many forces in our society. But when it comes to reforming and rehabilitating our prisoners it is becoming more and more evident that the most crucial job will have to be done by . . . prisoners. Inmate to inmate. Former inmate to inmate. The Fortune Society is only one of a number of organizations of ex-convicts engaged in this work.

Some time ago, the *New York Times* carried an article about Miguel Piñero, whose first play, *Short Eyes,* had "opened to rave reviews" at the New York Shakespeare Festival Public Theater. Piñero, so the article went, "is a former convict who has spent seven of his twenty-seven years in prison. Before he became a playwright, he was a burglar, mugger, shoplifter, drug addict and drug seller." After describing Piñero's life story, the reporter mentioned his desire to help those in prison, and quoted him as saying: "I want to set up programs where guys like myself can give something. We identify. . . . They can say 'Here comes a brother from the joint.' We're on the same level."[6] The same is true of drug addicts who are helped by former drug addicts through the exhausting experience of withdrawal and rehabilitation. Those who have suffered through the pain of that agony are best able to give help to those who are faced with that pain. Only he who has suffered can be a comforter, because he has been there himself.

Were you to imagine that drunk lying in the gutter and that prisoner when he was committing rape and that drug addict when she was shooting it up, you would get a picture worthy of Dante's hell. But that was before their transformation, before their Easter, before their death and resurrection.

These people did not become counselors and helpers and guides and comforters in spite of what they had done and in spite of what they had been, but because of what they had done and because of what they had been. Their corruption became incorruption, their dishonor glory, their weakness power, not because the normal course of events makes these transformations inevitable, but because there is a wondrous course of events that makes these transformations possible.

These men and women were transformed, not in spite of what they were but as the result of the death of what they were. They experienced in their lives the grace of death and resurrection.

20

※

Renewal and Transformation

A generation goes, and a generation comes but the earth
remains for ever. . . .
What has been is what will be, and what has been done is
what will be done; and there is nothing new under the sun.
ECCLESIASTES 1:4,9

The new does not appear from a collection of the elements
of the old. . . . When the new comes the old must disappear. . . . Out of the death of the old the new arises.
PAUL TILLICH, *The Shaking of the Foundations*[1]

Much has been written about our society's inability to accept
death as a fact of life. We celebrate life in a thousand ways
but we try to ignore death. Death is the negative, the un-
toward. Death is the enemy of life and has to be fought with
all means at our disposal. And when, in the end, we lose the
fight, we are loath to admit it and we encourage our mor-
ticians to camouflage death's pallor with the illusion of life.
To many, death is an embarrassing anachronistic remnant of
a technically primitive past, something that does not belong
in our advanced society. And when we read that the latest
statistics show a lengthening of our life expectancy, that we
are eking out of eternity another two or three or five years
for the average person to live, we rejoice: death, we say, we
are on our way; one of these days we will still conquer you

and recover that claim to immortality we forfeited in Paradise.

There never was such a claim. Immortality could not have been forfeited by us because it had never been given to us. Adam and Eve were mortal from the day they were created. They were just as mortal before they ate from the tree of knowledge as they were afterward. Only, before, they were not aware of it. They lived innocently as the animals live, "in the present, in the eternity of the instant."[2] Afterward, however, they knew what their fate was going to be. For the knowledge of good and evil enabled them to visualize various potential realities; it implied consciousness. And consciousness implies the knowledge of time, and time the knowledge of death.

We may feel that their knowledge of death was sufficient to bring an end to their paradisiacal bliss. Still, Adam and Eve were not expelled from Eden because they had eaten from the tree of knowledge. Though some may not remember this from their Sunday-school classes, there was a second tree, the tree of life. It was because he did not want them to eat from that second, less well-remembered, tree that God expelled them: "Behold, the man is become as one of us, knowing good and evil; and now, lest he put forth his hand and take also of the tree of life, and eat, and live for ever. . . . Therefore the Lord God sent him forth from the garden of Eden." This is how the ancient in our tradition symbolically expressed the truth that without death we would not be human, that death is essential to our humanity, that human life exists by the grace of human death. "There is no life except by death"—these words of the poet Walter Chalmers Smith are a modern restatement of that same truth.[3]

But one thing can be said of all times: the more we love

life, the less we are afraid of death; the more we are conscious of death, the more we are conscious of life, and to the degree to which we ignore death, we ignore life.

I know a family—husband, wife, and two children—an average family who lived an average life until one day when the mother had to have a cancer operation. She pulled through, but the doctors told her that there might be a recurrence. That operation took place several years ago. You might think that in the absence of a turn for the worse that average family has resumed its average life. But that is not so at all. The uncertainty with which they live and the threat of death it entails have made the marriage more vital, much warmer, much more focused on the essentials of life. The relationship of the parents with the children has become a deeper one; it has the glow of the spirit and of that extreme simplicity, which in the words of Stephen Spender, underlies

all causes and all appearances . . . like that of a lost child or a sick person. What really mattered were extreme situations, in the light of which ordinary ones should be judged: the beginning of creation, the end of the world, extreme poverty or suffering, great love, death. Life acquired significance . . . insofar as isolated moments of living were stretched upon these extremes, penetrated by the awareness of ultimate ends.[4]

It is this significance that the life of that family acquired. It is the significance to which George Eliot referred in a letter written to Sara Hennel on November 22, 1861. "The years seem to rush by now," the letter reads, "and I think of death as a fast approaching end of a journey: double and treble reason for loving, as well as working, while it is day."[5] It is the significance that stems from the realization that our days do not go on and on in an unclimactic, endless continuity, but that the days of our lives are limited. In the 90th Psalm we read: "Teach us to number our days, that we may apply our hearts unto wisdom." Our days are numbered. Somehow we hope, we expect, to live many more days. But we are wrong if we believe that the length of life is more important than the quality of life. And that quality can only be measured from the point of view of death. Betsey Barton expresses this thought when she describes how she cared for her mother during a long terminal illness:

There is a strange heightening of life that takes place if we live within the sight of a long dying. It lends an acute, sometimes agonizing pain and beauty to each moment that we are aware of it. It is like standing with a foot in two kinds of streams. One is made up of grocery bills and egos and servicing the car and public speeches. The other is made up of tenderness and yearning and nostalgia, for we know not what, and love in its fullest sense, and, finally, of the widest deeps and stretches of the spirit.

To live like this, aware of both streams and to see them intermingle . . . is to live the way the saints live all the time, perhaps —holding up the finiteness of their being to the infinite burning glass of eternity and of God.[6]

The very young know neither the agony nor the nostalgia that death can lend to life. Many years ago I overheard a five-year-old girl explain death to her four-year-old sister: "Death is nothing to be afraid of. It is just as if you were invited somewhere, and it is getting late, and you go to the hostess and you say, "Thank you for the wonderful party, I really enjoyed myself, but now it is time to go home.' "

Time to go home. She had not read the book of Ecclesiastes, which quotes an old sage as saying, "man goeth to his long home, and the mourners go about the streets"; she had not read the poet's words, "we feel a longing for the moment when our spirit shall be called home," or what President John Kennedy wrote about his brother Joe: "Death to him was less a setting forth than a returning." For since she was only five years old, she was not able to read at all. But with the poets and the prophets she had caught a glimpse of the truth that we are children of eternity and that life on earth is but a phase in the continuing life of the spirit.

Why is it that the years that bring us closer to death seem to make many of us less, rather than more, willing to accept its inevitability? Why is it that most of us keep pushing the thought of our death into the future, away from us?

Freud once observed that "our own death is indeed unimaginable and whenever we make an attempt to imagine it, we can perceive that we really survive as spectators." Two thousand years before him, Antiphanes had said, "No one ever died who was ready to die."

These views are not in accordance with those held by the church, which proclaims that "in the midst of life we are in death." What the little girl said to her sister fits into this great tradition of the church.

Jesus's equation of losing one's life with finding it is echoed by Goethe in a poem in which he speaks of dying and becoming: whoever has not experienced what it means "to die and to become," to die and to be re-created in dying, in his words, "is but a sorry vagrant on this dark earth of ours."[7] To realize that it is from the perspective of death that life derives its depth, that death creates life and is, in turn, overcome by it, that is what the Easter story is about.

Easter is not just a spring festival. There is every reason to be joyful upon the return of the good season after the hardship of winter, but there is no newness in it. Spring, recurring annually, repeats itself. This spring is as last spring was and as next spring will be. It is the repetitiousness described by the Preacher:

The sun rises and the sun goes down . . . round and round goes the wind. . . .
   All things are full of weariness. . . .
   What has been is what will be . . . and there is nothing new under the sun. . . .
   Is there a thing of which it is said See, this is new?

This desperate rhetorical question, by which present-day existentialists are still (or, should I say, again?) haunted, is answered by Paul's description of the Easter happenings that finds its climax in the triumphant exclamation "the old has passed away, behold, the new has come." The Easter celebration of the new that has come is the very antithesis of a spring festival. For we do not celebrate at Easter the beginning of another cycle in the endless routine of changing seasons, but the breaking of the routine, the opening up of a new dimension, a dimension of the spirit which knows no routine. At Easter we celebrate the truth that there *is* spiritual newness under the sun, newness that can break the vicious circle, newness that enables us to overcome death with life, hatred with love, division with wholeness.

For it is not true that a person who is divided within himself is doomed to remain divided. It is not true that husband and wife who have failed each other are doomed to continue to fail each other. It is not true that, when people who are united in community at some time lose their sense of unity and love and responsibility toward each other, the results are bound to haunt them forever. For in newness of spirit we can and must forgive each other and ourselves, so that indeed the old may pass away and the new may come.

But the old may be stubborn. It may be hard to get rid of it. Because in order to get rid of the old there has to be a dying. "Out of the death of the old the new arises," says Tillich.[8] "Die and become," said Goethe.[9]

It is hard to die. It is hard to give up. It is hard to let go.

I had a conversation with a twenty-year-old boy. At his age he should have been a man, but he was a boy. He knew it and suffered from it. His inability to grow up was the very topic of our conversation. Therapy had been suggested to him but he had said no, he did not want to go into therapy because he "was afraid to lose his identity." He was afraid to die.

Religious fanatics brought forth the medieval legend of Ahasuerus, the Jew who was condemned to wander the earth until the day of judgment. In their hatred of the people they regarded as the murderers of Christ, they inflicted upon their legendary victim the worst of all curses: they denied him the right to die. Until their secular descendants killed him at Auschwitz. Then something strange happened. For one might say with some validity that his death brought about the state of Israel, that Tel Aviv is Auschwitz resurrected, that the death in despair has somehow brought forth the life in hope.

My young friend is resisting this transformation; he is afraid to die. If he does not learn to accept death, there will be no resurrection for him. He will make himself into some kind of Ahasuerus. Because the renewal in us is not an automatic renewal; it does not happen in a cyclical way, like spring, but depends on our desire for renewal, our willingness to die and to overcome our dying in the resurrection as a transformed being, a being with a new identity.

[179]

This is what the first Passover celebrated: when the Israelites left Egypt, they left the old behind; their old identity of
slaves sitting around the fat pots of Egypt was transformed
into that of free wanderers in the barren Sinai desert.

And what about Jesus? From the synoptic gospels, it is
clear that nothing would have happened if he had not chosen
to go to Jerusalem. Even so, he had to direct the drama of his
capture and death and, until the last moment, when he appeared before Pilate, he could have saved his life by answering a few simple questions. "And he answered him never a
word," as Matthew says. For Jesus wanted to fulfill the pre-
dictions of the prophets, of Isaiah and Jeremiah, of the
Psalms and the book of Daniel; the prophets who wrote the
part of the messiah centuries before one appeared who was
willing to pick up the script and assume the part, the part of
the man who dies in ignominy and is resurrected in glory.

Few if any liberals believe in the physical resurrection. We
are not alone. Reinhold Niebuhr, in emphasizing the importance of the symbolical meaning of the resurrection, states
that "the idea of the resurrection of the body can of course
not be literally true."[10]

Paul Tillich goes even further when he refers to the women
who found the tomb empty on Easter morning:

The sources of this story are rather late and questionable, and
there is no indication of it in the earliest tradition. . . . Theo-
logically speaking, it is a rationalization of the event, interpreting
it with physical categories that identify resurrection with . . .
the presence or absence of a physical body. Then the absurd
question arises as to what happened to the molecules which com-
prise the corpse of Jesus of Nazareth. Then absurdity becomes
compounded into blasphemy.[11]

Agreement on the nonliteralness of the resurrection does not necessarily mean agreement on its symbolic meaning. It can still mean different things to different people. To me the resurrection has two distinct symbolic meanings, which supplement and ultimately merge into one another.

First, the resurrection symbolizes death's transforming power, the birth of the new out of the death of the old. This interpretation gives us the key to the spiritual growth that can take place within us. It consists of our ability to die and to be reborn, to be transformed and to be renewed many times during our life. My young friend lacked this ability. Many people do. They are unable to grow. They don't grow up.

Very few of us are wholly grown up. Most of us have been unable to let go of certain childish attitudes that conflict with our otherwise adult lives. It means that some part of our being did not die and was not reborn; our death and resurrection have been incomplete; a part of us got stuck somewhere in childhood and did not grow with the remainder of our personality and causes us pain.

Still, most of us have time and again experienced that dying which André Maurois alluded to when he said: "partir c'est mourir un peu" ("to leave is to die a little bit"). To leave home, to leave college, to leave middle age, to be prepared to leave life, but also to give up illusions, to let go the unfulfilled hope, to suffer hurt pride, and, even more, to accept the loss of loved ones, to accept defeat and failure, and to realize that in the acceptance lies the victory of resurrection. Let's face it: Jesus's life *was* one big failure, and victory resulted from his acceptance thereof—yes, from his having sought that failure.

The story of Jesus's life and death and resurrection thus

[181]

symbolizes the process of spiritual growth that goes on within us as individuals.

How well he knew it: "For whosoever will save his life [that is, cling to his old identity] shall lose it: and whosoever will lose his life for my sake [that is, for the sake of my cause, the cause of death and resurrection as transformation and renewal] shall find it."

In order to live, we must be willing to die. And if we are willing to die, if we are willing to let go, we may experience the resurrection.

The symbolism of the Easter event thus points to the resurrection all of us can experience during our life.

The second symbolic meaning points to the experience of the resurrection of one man after his death. Its nature was made clear at Pentecost: it was the resurrection of his spirit within his followers.

Thus Paul cried out: "Not I but Christ liveth in me." Thus Angelus Silezius, the sixteenth-century German mystic, wrote:

> Should Christ be born a thousand times anew,
> Despair, O man, unless he's born in you![12]

And the same thought was expressed by that great Unitarian Albert Schweitzer when he wrote

The truth is, it is not Jesus as historically known, but Jesus as spiritually arisen within men, who is significant for our time and can help it. Not the historical Jesus, but the spirit which goes forth from Him and in the spirits of men strives for new influence and rule, is that which overcomes the world. . . . The abiding and eternal in Jesus . . . can only be understood by contact with His spirit which is still at work in the world.[13]

That spirit is at work when an orphan is adopted, when a juvenile delinquent is rehabilitated, and when an unwed mother is protected from being ostracized. It is at work when the sick and the dying are comforted, when the hungry are fed and the naked are clothed.

That spirit is at work whenever power restrains itself and violence is tempered, whenever moderation prevails over excessiveness and forgiveness over vengeance, and, above all, whenever love overcomes hatred.

This, to me, is the true sense of the resurrection and at the same time the deepest meaning of Easter. It takes whatever happened on that Sunday morning two thousand years ago out of the sphere of the miraculous and brings it into the sphere of the mysterious, and that is where it belongs. For what confronts us is not the fact of a unique, magic resurrection outside of us, but the possibility of renewing ourselves by making complete the resurrection within us. And in striving to make it complete we must overcome our greed and our jealousies, our anxieties and our selfishness, our vanity and our lust for power. For that resurrection within us, that great renewal, must be preceded by the dying of the ego-self. It is a matter of life and death, of death and continuing life; it is a matter of overcoming the old and embracing the new; it is a matter of stepping out of our biological darkness into the light of the Spirit.

NOTES

Notes

EPIGRAPH

1. Elie Wiesel, *The Gates of the Forest,* trans. Frances Frenaye (New York: Avon Books, 1967), pp. 7–10.

1. THE MASK OF RELIGION

1. Michael Novak, *A Time to Build* (New York: Macmillan Co., 1967), p. 313.
2. Archibald MacLeish, *J.B.* (Boston: Houghton Mifflin Co., 1958), p. 23–24.
3. *Ibid.,* pp. 95–97.
4. Mircea Eliade, *No Souvenirs: Journal, 1957–1969* (New York: Harper & Row, 1977), p. 38.
5. Leonard Bernstein, *The Unanswered Question* (Cambridge, Mass.: Harvard University Press, 1976), pp. 375–376.
6. *Ibid.,* p. 377.
7. Friedrich Nietzsche, *Jenseit von Gut und Böse* (Leipzig: C. G. Naumann, 1899), p. 60, my translation.
8. Quoted in Carl D. Schneider, *Shame, Exposure, and Privacy* (Boston: Beacon Press, 1977), p. 7.
9. *Ibid.,* p. 8.
10. Sallie TeSelle, *Speaking in Parables* (Philadelphia: Fortress Press, 1975), pp. 40, 114.
11. James Luther Adams, "The Lure of Persuasion: Some Themes from Whitehead," *The Unitarian Universalist Christian,* vol. 30, no. 4 (Winter, 1975–1976), p. 11.
12. e.e. cummings, *I x I* , "XVI," in *Complete Poems: 1913–1962* (New York: Harcourt Brace Jovanovich, 1968), p. 556.
13. Carl D. Schneider, *Shame, Exposure, and Privacy,* p. 117.

2. THE REAL AND THE TRUE

1. Loren Eiseley, "The Cosmic Orphan," *Saturday Review/World,* February 23, 1974, p. 16.
2. *De Carne Christi* 5.23.
3. Paul Tillich, "The Lost Dimension in Religion," *Saturday Evening Post,* June 14, 1958, p. 29 ff.
4. J. Robert Oppenheimer, *Science and the Common Understanding* (New York: Simon & Schuster, 1953), pp. 6, 40.
5. *Ibid.,* p. 69.
6. Albert Schweitzer, *The Quest of the Historical Jesus: A Critical Study of its Progress from Reimarus to Wrede,* trans. W. Montgomery (New York: Macmillan Co., 1968), p. 401.

3. THE COSMIC AND THE COSMETIC

1. Grace Hechinger, "The Insidious Pollution of Language," *Wall Street Journal,* October 27, 1971.
2. James Reston, *New York Times,* March 27, 1974.
3. Michael Novak, *Ascent of the Mountain, Flight of the Dove* (New York: Harper & Row, 1971), p. 108.
4. Quoted in Christopher Lasch, *The Culture of Narcissism: American Life in an Age of Diminishing Expectations* (New York: W. W. Norton & Co., 1979), p. 6.
5. J. I. Simmons and Barry Winograd, *It's Happening: A Portrait of the Youth Scene Today* (Santa Barbara, Calif.: Marc-Laird Publications, 1966), p. 85.
6. *Ibid.,* p. 172.
7. *Ibid.*
8. Jane Howard, *Please Touch: A Guided Tour of the Human Potential Movement* (New York: McGraw-Hill Book Co., 1970; New York: Dell Publishing Co., A Delta Book, 1971).
9. Robert C. Ouradnik, "The Middle-Class Quest for Alternatives," *The Christian Century,* April 3, 1974, p. 366.
10. *Ibid.,* pp. 366–367.
11. "The Devil and the Flesh," produced by Marilyn Grabowski, photographed by Alexas Urba, *Playboy,* May 1974. How Eros got into the act is not quite clear, and his legitimacy in the underworld is doubtful, as is the description of the underworld (Hell? Hades?) as "sensuous."

4. THE HEDGEHOG AND THE FOX

1. Helen Keller, *Midstream* (New York: Doubleday, Doran & Co., 1929), p. 333.
2. Michael Novak, *Ascent of the Mountain, Flight of the Dove*, p. 43.
3. Isaiah Berlin, *The Hedgehog and the Fox: An Essay on Tolstoy's View of History* (New York: Simon & Schuster, 1966), pp. 7–8.
4. Thomas à Kempis, *Of the Imitation of Christ* (London: Oxford University Press, 1900), vol. I, pp. 5–6.
5. Henry Brooks Adams, *The Education of Henry Adams* (New York: Random House, Modern Library, 1931), p. 498.
6. See Arthur Koestler, *The Sleepwalkers: A History of Man's Changing Vision of the Universe* (New York: Macmillan Co., 1959; Baltimore: Penguin Books, 1964).
7. Pitirim A. Sorokin, *Society, Culture, and Personality: Their Structure and Dynamics* (New York: Harper & Brothers, 1947), pp. 345, 348.
8. e. e. cummings, *Complete Poems*, p. 609.
9. *Hymns of the Spirit* (Boston: Beacon Press, 1937), p. 12.
10. Thomas à Kempis, *Of the Imitation of Christ*, p. 3.
11. J. Robert Oppenheimer, *Science and the Common Understanding*, p. 89.
12. Letter by Gustave Flaubert, in Carl Michalson, *The Hinge of History* (New York: Charles Scribner's Sons, 1959), introduction.
13. Goethe, *Faust*, trans. George Madison Priest (New York: Alfred A. Knopf, 1950), Part I, lines 355, 382–383.
14. Luigi Pirandello, *Right You are (If You Think So)*, in *Three Plays* trans. Arthur Livingston (New York: E. P. Dutton, 1922).
15. Walter Kaufmann, *The Faith of a Heretic* (Garden City, N.Y.: Doubleday & Co., 1961), p. 81.
16. Pitirim A. Sorokin, *Society, Culture, and Personality*, p. 355.

5. CONTINUITY OR DISCONTINUITY

1. Paul Goodman, *New Reformation* (New York: Random House, 1970), p. 85.
2. Christopher Lasch, *The Culture of Narcissism*, p. 68.
3. Quoted in Arthur Koestler, *The Sleepwalkers*, p. 358.
4. Quoted in Loren Eiseley, *All The Strange Hours* (New York: Charles Scribner's Sons, 1975), p. 192.

5. William James, *Pragmatism: A New Name for Some Old Ways of Thinking* (New York: Longmans Green & Co., 1909), p. 78.
6. Michael Novak, *All the Catholic People* (New York: Herder and Herder, 1971), p. 51.
7. *Zygon, Journal of Religion & Science*, vol. I, no. 1 (March 1966), p. 7.
8. Robert N. Bellah, *The Broken Covenant: American Civil Religion in Time of Trial* (New York: Seabury Press, 1975), p. 4.
9. Lewis Mumford, *The Pentagon of Power: The Myth of the Machine* (New York: Harcourt Brace Jovanovich, 1970), pp. 403–404.
10. *New York Times*, November 17, 1971.
11. Harvey Cox, *The Feast of Fools* (Cambridge, Mass.: Harvard University Press, 1969), p. 33.
12. Quoted in Theodosius Dobzhansky, "Evolution: Implications for Religion," *The Christian Century*, July 19, 1967, p. 941.
13. J. Robert Nelson, "End-of-Summer Thoughts on the End of Christianity," *The Christian Century*, September 20, 1978, p. 845.
14. Donald Szantho Harrington, "The Faith Beneath Freedom," *The Unitarian Christian*, vol. 23, no. 2 (Summer 1967), pp. 10–11.
15. *Ibid.*

6. BETWEEN THE SILENCES

1. Friedrich Nietzsche, *Also Sprach Zarathustra* (Leipzig: E. G. Nauman, 1899), p. 471, my translation.
2. Joseph Lelyveld, "The Story of a Soldier Who Refused to Fire at Songmy," *New York Times Magazine*, December 14, 1969, p. 114.
3. Viktor E. Frankl, *Man's Search for Meaning: An Introduction to Logotherapy*, rev. ed. (Boston: Beacon Press, 1962), pp. 120–121.
4. *Ibid.*, p. 120.
5. *New York Times*, October 6, 1969, p. 28.

7. THE BURDEN OF KNOWING

1. Dorothee Sölle, *Lijden* (Baarn, Netherlands: Uitgeverij Bosch & Keuning, 1973), p. 34, my translation.
2. Richard L. Rubenstein, *The Cunning of History* (New York: Harper & Row, Harper Colophon Books, 1975), p. 100.
3. Rollo May, *Man's Search for Himself* (New York: W. W. Norton & Co., 1953), pp. 85–86.

4. Martin Buber, *Between Man and Man,* trans. Ronald Gregor Smith (New York: Macmillan Co., 1948), p. 132.

5. Walt Whitman, "Song of Myself," *Leaves of Grass* (New York: Aventine Press, 1931), p. 61.

6. Eliot, T. S., "Choruses from 'The Rock'," *Collected Poems, 1909–1962* (New York: Harcourt , Brace & World, 1963), p. 147.

7. William Barrett, *Irrational Man: A Study in Existential Philosophy* (Garden City, N.Y.: Doubleday & Co., 1958), p. 21.

8. *Ibid.,* p. 21–22.

9. "XII," *The Collected Poems of A. E. Housman* (New York: Henry Holt, 1940), p. 111.

10. Jacquetta Hawkes, "Nine Tantalizing Mysteries of Nature," *New York Times Sunday Magazine,* July 7, 1957, p. 5.

11. Michael Novak, *The Experience of Nothingness* (New York: Harper & Row, Harper Colophon Books, 1970), p. 26.

8. THE WILLINGNESS TO SUFFER

1. André Malraux, *The Voices of Silence* (Garden City, N.Y.: Doubleday & Co., 1953), pp. 281–282.

2. Michael Stolpman, in Elizabeth Kübler-Ross, *To Live Until We Say Good-Bye* (Englewood Cliffs, N.J.: Prentice-Hall, 1978), p. 139.

3. Erich Fromm, *You Shall Be as Gods* (New York: Holt, Rinehart and Winston, 1966), p. 92.

4. Dorothee Sölle, *Lijden,* p. 70.

5. Dr. J. H. van den Berg, *Metabletica of Leer der Veranderingen* (Nijkerk, Netherlands: C. F. Callenbach, 1957), p. 101, my translation.

6. Viktor E. Frankl, *Man's Search for Meaning,* p. 115.

7. *Ibid.,* p. 76.

8. *Ibid.,* pp. 78, 79, 65.

9. Jacques Lusseyran, *And There Was Light,* trans. Elizabeth R. Cameron (Boston: Little, Brown & Co., 1963), p. 283.

10. Viktor E. Frankl, *Man's Search for Meaning,* p. 137.

11. Elie Wiesel, *A Jew Today* (New York: Random House, 1978), p. 199.

12. Abel J. Herzberg, *Amor Fati* (Amsterdam: Em. Querido's Uitgeverij, 1977), p. 124, my translation.

13. Arnold Toynbee, *An Historian's Approach to Religion* (New York: Oxford University Press, 1956), p. 5.

14. André Malraux, *The Voices of Silence,* p. 282.

15. Albert Schweitzer, *On the Edge of the Primeval Forest,* trans. C. T. Campion (New York: Macmillan Co., 1931), p. 173.
16. Miguel Unamuno, *The Tragic Sense of Life,* trans. Anthony Nerrigen (Princeton: Princeton University Press, 1972), p. 224.

9. THE MYSTERY OF REDEMPTION

1. Archibald MacLeish, *J.B.,* p. 89.
2. Cf. Milan Machoveč, *A Marxist Looks at Jesus* (Philadelphia: Fortress Press, 1976), p. 182.
3. Dag Hammarskjöld, *Markings,* trans. Leif Sjöberg and W. H. Auden (New York: Alfred A. Knopf, 1964), p. 198.
4. Monica Hellwig, "Christian Theology and the Covenant of Israel," *Journal of Ecumenical Studies,* vol. 7, no. 1 (Winter 1970), p. 49.
5. Sr. Charlotte Klein, "Catholics and Jews—Ten Years After Vatican II," *Jews and Christians in Dialogue,* ed. Leonard Swidler, *Journal of Ecumenical Studies,* Special Issue, vol. 12, no. 4 (Fall 1975), pp. 480–481.
6. *Disputations and Dialogue: Readings in the Jewish-Christian Encounter,* ed. F. E. Talmage (New York: Ktav Publishing House, 1975), pp. 84–85.
7. Sr. Charlotte Klein, p. 482.
8. Walter Muehl, "The Myth of Self-Evident Truth," *The Christian Century,* November 2, 1977, p. 1000.
9. Siegfried Sassoon, "On Passing the New Menin Gate," *Collected Poems* (London: Faber and Faber, 1961), p. 188.
10. *New York Times,* November 11, 1977, p. A29.
11. *Ibid.*
12. Arthur R. Butz, *The Hoax of the Twentieth Century* (Chapel Ascote, Ladbroke, Southam, Warwickshire: Historical Press, 1976), p. 7.
13. Lawrence L. Langer, *The Holocaust and the Literary Imagination* (New Haven and London: Yale University Press, 1975), pp. 84–85.
14. Elie Wiesel, *Night,* trans. Stella Rodway (New York: Hill and Wang, 1960), p. 71.

10. THE COURAGE TO BE A FAILURE

1. Martin Buber, *Israel and the World: Essays in a Time of Crisis* (New York: Schocken Books, 1948), pp. 117–118.

2. Lewis Thomas, *The Medusa and the Snail* (New York: Viking Press, 1979), p. 39.
3. Vance Packard, *The Status Seekers* (New York: David McKay Co., 1959), p. 199.
4. *New York Times,* June 26, 1979, p. T1.
5. Erich Fromm, *Psychoanalysis and Religion* (New Haven: Yale University Press, 1956), pp. 101–102.
6. *Ibid.,* p. 102.
7. David Lawrence, *New York Herald Tribune,* April 1, 1960. Many years later, weirdly echoing these words, Yasir Arafat, head of the Palestine Liberation Organization, reacted to the progress made on the Egyptian-Israeli peace treaty with this comment: "We don't turn the other cheek, we slap back twice as hard," *New York Times,* March 15, 1979.

11. A BARGAIN WITH GOD

1. Hermann Hesse, *Demian: The Story of Emil Sinclair's Youth,* trans. Michael Roloff and Michael Lebeck (New York: Harper & Row, 1965), pp. 108, 125.
2. Dag Hammarskjöld, *Markings,* p. 56.
3. John A. T. Robinson, *The New Reformation?* (London: SCM Press, 1965), p. 113.
4. John F. Hayward, *Existentialism and Religious Liberalism* (Boston: Beacon Press, 1962), p. 27.
5. "Camus at Stockholm: The Acceptance of the Nobel Prize," trans. Justin O'Brien, *The Atlantic Monthly,* May 1958, pp. 33–34.
6. Albert Camus, *The Rebel: An Essay on Man in Revolt,* rev. and trans. by Anthony Bower (New York: Vintage Books, 1958), p. 304.

12. EXCEPT THOU BLESS ME

1. Paul Tillich, *Systematic Theology* (Chicago: University of Chicago Press 1957–63), vol. II, p. 71.
2. *New York Times,* November 16, 1974, p. 35.
3. Robert Frost, *In the Clearing* (New York: Holt, Rinehart and Winston, 1962), p. 39.
4. Albert Camus, *The Plague,* trans. Stuart Gilbert (New York: Alfred A. Knopf, 1948), pp. 195–196.

5. Peter L. Berger, *A Rumor of Angels: Modern Society and the Rediscovery of the Supernatural* (Garden City, N.Y.: Doubleday & Co., 1969), p. 31.
6. *Ibid.*
7. Israel Shenker, *New York Times,* June 9, 1974.
8. William James, *The Varieties of Religious Experience* (New York: Random House, 1902), p. 161.
9. Peter L. Berger, *A Rumor of Angels,* p. 32.

13. AS A TALE THAT IS TOLD

1. Michael Novak, *Ascent of the Mountain, Flight of the Dove,* pp. 46–47.
2. Henry David Thoreau, *Walden* (Princeton: Princeton University Press, 1971), p. 135.
3. Loren Eiseley, *The Immense Journey* (New York: Random House, 1957), pp. 120–121.
4. Winston S. Churchill, *Their Finest Hour* (Boston: Houghton Mifflin Co., 1949), p. 226.
5. James Reston, *New York Times,* July 26, 1974.
6. Hilary Ng'weno, "The Panthers: An African View," *New York Times,* October 2, 1970, p. 35.
7. Steven Kelman, *Push Comes to Shove: The Escalation of Student Protest* (Boston: Houghton Mifflin Co., 1970), pp. 147–148.
8. Thornton Wilder, *Our Town: A Play in Three Acts* (New York: Harper and Row, 1957), pp. 98–100.

14. ON GIVING THANKS

1. Rainer Maria Rilke, *Man and God,* ed. Victor Gollancz (Boston: Houghton Mifflin Co., 1951), p. 89.
2. Henry Alford, "Come, ye thankful people, come," 1844, *Hymns of the Spirit* (Boston: Beacon Press, 1937), p. 141.
3. William Shakespeare, *King Henry VI, Part II,* Act I, Scene 1, line 19.

15. BE STILL, AND KNOW

1. Sören Kierkegaard, quoted in Arthur Foote, *Taking Down the Defenses: A Lenten Manual for 1954* (Boston: Beacon Press, 1954), p. 11.

2. e. e. cummings, *Complete Poems*, p. 844.

3. John Greenleaf Whittier, "Dear Lord and Father of Mankind," *Hymns of the Spirit* (Boston: Beacon Press, 1937), p. 250.

4. William Shakespeare, *King Henry IV, Part II*, Act I, Scene 2, line 139.

5. Jacques Lusseyran, *Le Monde Commence Aujourd'hui* (Paris: La Table Ronde, Denoel, 1960).

6. Simone Weil, *Waiting for God* (New York: G. P. Putnam & Sons, 1951), p. 124.

7. Richard Fleckno, *Poems of All Sorts*, 1653, quoted in Charles Lamb, *The Complete Works and Letters of Charles Lamb* (New York: Random House, Modern Library, 1935), p. 41.

8. Quoted in Philip Hewett, *The Uncarven Image: A Manual for Meditation* (Boston: Beacon Press, 1962), p. vi.

9. Thomas à Kempis, *Of the Imitation of Christ*, p. 38.

16. THE BRIGHTER LIGHT

1. World Development Report, World Bank, 1978, quoted in *The Economist*, August 19–25, 1978, pp. 63–64.

2. Quoted in David Riesman, *The Lonely Crowd* (New Haven: Yale University Press, 1961), p. 83.

3. Gertrude Crampton, *Tootle* (New York: Simon & Schuster, Little Golden Library, 1945).

17. A HEAVENLY OR AN EARTHLY KINGDOM

1. Rebecca West, *Black Lamb and Grey Falcon* (New York: Viking Press, 1941), pp. 910–911. Tsar Lazar commanded the Serbian army that was defeated by the invading Ottoman Turks at Kossovo in the year 1389.

2. *Ibid.*, p. 911.

3. John W. Gardner, *Self-Renewal: The Individual and the Innovative Society* (New York: Harper & Row, Harper Colophon Books, 1964), p. 62.

4. *New York Times*, November 3, 1970.

5. Michael Novak, *A Time to Build*, p. 4.

18. THE VERTICAL AND THE HORIZONTAL

1. James Luther Adams, *On Being Human Religiously, Selected Essays in Religion and Society*, ed. Max L. Stackhouse (Boston: Beacon Press, 1976), p. 150. Blumhardt was a late nineteenth-century German Lutheran pastor.

2. Christiane Desroches-Noblecourt, *Tutankhamen: Life and Death of a Pharaoh* (New York: New York Graphic Society, 1976), p. 84.

3. James Luther Adams, *On Being Human Religiously*, p. 92.

4. William Butler Yeats, *The Second Coming: Selected Poems and Two Plays of William Butler Yeats*, ed. M. L. Rosenthal (New York: Macmillan Co., 1962), p. 91.

5. Robert Kegan, *The Sweeter Welcome* (Needham Hts., Mass.: Humanitas Press, 1976), p. 9.

6. Dean Acheson, *Present at the Creation: My Years in the State Department* (New York: W. W. Norton & Co., 1969), p. 360.

7. William Butler Yeats, "The Circus Animals' Desertion," *The Second Coming*, p. 185.

8. *Ibid.*

19. SPRING, EXODUS, RESURRECTION

1. Paul Tillich, *The Shaking of the Foundations* (New York: Charles Scribner's Sons, 1948), pp. 181–182.

2. Sir James George Frazer, *The Golden Bough: A Study in Magic and Religion* (New York: Macmillan Co., 1940), p. 361.

3. Peter L. Berger, *The Sacred Canopy: Elements of a Sociological Theory of Religion* (New York: Doubleday & Co., 1969), p. 119.

4. Quoted in Paul Tillich, *Systematic Theology*, vol. II, p. 73.

5. Peter L. Berger, *The Sacred Canopy*, p. 167.

6. *New York Times*, March 27, 1974, pp. 45, 68.

20. RENEWAL AND TRANSFORMATION

1. Paul Tillich, *The Shaking of the Foundations*, p. 181.

2. Jorge Luis Borges, *A Personal Anthology* (New York: Grove Press, 1967), p. 19.

3. Walter Chalmers Smith, *Obrig Grange*, bk. 6, quoted in James Dalton, ed., *Masterpieces of Religious Verse* (New York: Harper & Row, 1948), p. 1357.

4. Stephen Spender, *World Within World* (Berkeley and Los Angeles: University of California Press, 1966), p. 335.
5. George Eliot, *The George Eliot Letters*, ed. Gordon S. Haight (New Haven: Yale University Press, 1954), vol. 3, p. 466.
6. Betsey Barton, *As Love Is Deep* (New York: Duell Sloan & Pearce, 1957), pp. 74–75.
7. Goethe, "Selige Sehnsucht," *West-Ostlicher Divan,* Buch des Sängers (Berlin: Der Tempel-Verlag, 1962), p. 895, my translation.
8. Paul Tillich, *The Shaking of the Foundations,* p. 181.
9. Goethe, "Selige Sehnsucht," p. 895.
10. Reinhold Niebuhr, *Beyond Tragedy* (New York: Charles Scribner's Sons, 1965), p. 290.
11. Paul Tillich, *Systematic Theology,* vol. II, pp. 155–156.
12. Victor Gollancz, *Man and God* (Boston: Houghton Mifflin Co., 1951), p. 45.
13. Albert Schweitzer, *The Quest of the Historical Jesus,* p. 399.

INDEX

Index

A Note About the Author

G. Peter Fleck, a Dutch-born investment banker who came to the United States after the occupation of his native country by the Nazis, is a distinguished layman of the Unitarian Universalist denomination. He has served as a member of the boards of trustees of the American Unitarian Association, the Unitarian Universalist Association, and as chairman of the board of the Meadville/Lombard Theological School in Chicago. He has preached in many churches and fellowships over the past twenty-five years and holds honorary doctorates from Thomas Starr King School for the Ministry, Berkeley, California, and Meadville/Lombard Theological School. He and his wife Ruth live on Cape Cod.

A Note About the Type

Composed in Linotype Baskerville by
American–Stratford Graphic Services, Inc.,
Brattleboro, Vermont.
Printed and bound by American Book–
Stratford Press, Inc., Saddlebrook, New Jersey.
Designed by Sidney Feinberg.